Experiments in Family Planning

Roberto Cuca and Catherine S. Pierce

Experiments in Family Planning

Lessons from the Developing World

Foreword by Bernard Berelson

Published for the World Bank
The Johns Hopkins University Press
Baltimore and London

The views and interpretations in this book are those of the authors and should not be attributed to the World Bank, to its affiliated organizations, or to any individual acting in their behalf.

Library of Congress Cataloging in Publication Data

Cuca, Roberto, 1940–
Experiments in family planning.
Bibliography: p. 247
1. Underdeveloped areas—Birth control.
I. Pierce, Catherine S., 1942– joint author.
II. Title.
HQ766.C9 362.8′2 77-4602
ISBN 0-8018-2013-8
ISBN 0-8018-2014-6 pbk.

Foreword

Rapid population growth in the developing nations emerged as a social problem of magnitude only after World War II; it was generally recognized as such within a decade or so and was being addressed on a broad international scale within another decade. By any historical standard that is a short time for the development of policies and programs for an issue as consequential, sensitive, and controversial as population growth.

The full story of the world's consideration of "the population problem" in the past few decades, or even the story of how scientific study fits into that consideration, remains to be told. But this volume by Roberto Cuca and Catherine Pierce does move in that direction by presenting a review of the "experiments" done to date on the delivery of family planning services (as the authors are careful to point out, the term requires quotation marks in this context).

In my judgment this review is comprehensive, concise, realistic, and balanced. It is comprehensive in its coverage of all the important studies that can be designated as experiments in family planning, no fewer than ninety-six efforts on six central subjects in nearly thirty countries. It is concise not only in its topical summaries of both substantive and methodological issues but in the valuable compendium of the experiments, in which key elements are succinctly and systematically described. It is realistic in evaluating the experiments not only by how they meet customary scientific criteria but also by how they fit into the unfolding process of policy formation. It is balanced in its appraisal of contributions and deficiencies, achievements and shortfalls.

The literature of population contains no similar array of experiments in family planning. Here they are set forth, warts and all, and their lessons drawn, not simply on how the past could and should have been different—how easy it is to play that game!—but mainly on the proper criteria and agenda for the future. The authors face up to the inevitable disappointments with what has been learned and to the inevitable compromises with technical correctness. Would the situation be improved today with fewer and better experiments? By scientific standards, probably yes; by policy standards, probably not. To some extent, quantity did war with quality in these years; yet policymakers were also pressing the requirements of demonstration, which many of the experiments really were. (As in Dr. Johnson's comment about women preaching and dogs walking on their hind legs, the question was not how well it could be done but whether it could be done at all!).

Cuca and Pierce conclude that "In a sector like family planning, the perfectly designed, rigorously implemented experiment is simply not possible," but at the same time that "Much of the knowledge about family planning delivery systems . . . was accumulated over the last twenty years through experimental efforts." It is to their credit that they do not limit themselves to the obvious scientific criticisms that can be made of such studies but inquire as well into their programmatic relevance: The conclusions of many experiments "cannot be viewed as definitive answers to the questions investigated. Nevertheless, experimentation has had a significant impact on the development of family planning delivery systems." It was often the doing itself that mattered as much as or more than the results; and more was learned from this effort than the experimental design might indicate.

This book is doubly rich in the way it conveys the contribution of science to policy: It is both a competent survey of the substance and techniques of the studies and a sensible interpretation of where they fit into the ongoing development of family planning policies. The wide-ranging literature from the significant period of 1960–75—nearly six completed experiments a year or one every two months—is here pulled together in exemplary fashion. Among other things, this volume demonstrates for other fields how the literature can be analyzed to illustrate policy issues still very much alive.

The work of Cuca and Pierce was done at the World Bank as part of its effort to promote development and improve human welfare in the poorer countries of the world. The Bank has determined that slowing rates of population growth is crucial to these concerns and has allocated resources to social research on the problem. In the nature of the case, the Bank's contribution to the total research enterprise carried on in universities and institutes around the world must necessarily be small in size; but given its central and prestigious position within the development system, its contribution to responsible consideration of causes and consequences, of the nature of the problem and what can be done about it, can be and indeed has been substantial. Publication of this study adds to the Bank's contribution a critical but, in the original sense, appreciative review of a whole stream of work that played a major part in shaping the recent course of action on the population problem. This volume can provide guidance not only to the Bank's own effort—its initial purpose—but to the efforts of the entire field.

It has been observed that the worldwide effort to provide people with safe and effective fertility-regulating methods has probably generated more social science research than any directed change program in history. Whether that is literally so or not, there has been a considerable amount of research, and this volume presents a welcome appraisal of one major sector.

Bernard Berelson
President Emeritus and Senior Fellow,
The Population Council
Chairman, External Advisory Panel
on Population, The World Bank

October 1977

Contents

TABLES

Preface

IN RECENT YEARS the World Bank has been engaged in an analysis of the growing international experience in family planning programs. It is hoped that the lessons derived from such analyses will be useful for improving both national family planning programs and family planning projects sponsored by the Bank in developing countries. An earlier World Bank publication, *Population Policies and Economic Development*, examined the interrelation between population growth and development and summarized the status of work on particular issues. The authors drew a number of policy conclusions, based on a comparative analysis of national family planning programs.[1] The present book focuses on the process through which new knowledge is generated. It evaluates the usefulness of experimental efforts in family planning services and attempts to devise guidelines for future experimentation in this field.

Within the last twenty years there have been extensive experimental efforts in the developing world to determine more effective ways of providing family planning services. Researchers and managers interested in family planning

1. Timothy King and others, *Population Policies and Economic Development* (Baltimore: Johns Hopkins University Press, 1974).

were dissatisfied with the results of ongoing family planning programs, but they realized that the initiation of totally new delivery systems or even major modifications would involve both risk and expense. In an experimental framework, however, innovative techniques and different inputs can be tested on a limited scale before being incorporated in a regular program. The results of such experiments have thus often indicated what approaches should be adopted or discarded to enhance the effectiveness and efficiency of family planning programs.

The staff and consultants of the Population Council have done considerable work in disseminating the findings of many family planning experiments.[2] John Ross's *Findings from Family Planning Research* (1972), Dorothy Nortman's annual *Factbook*, and others of the council's Reports on Population/Family Planning provide much information pertaining to both family planning programs and experimental efforts. John Ross's study and Albert M. Marckwardt's *Latin American Supplement* reviewed the results of family planning research and presented detailed accounts of the research design employed, the nature of the intervention, and the findings. In assessing the relative impact of population programs as opposed to socioeconomic change, Ross and his colleagues concluded that programs were the more significant factor in reducing fertility—even in Taiwan where modernization has been very rapid.[3]

Elizabeth T. Hilton and Arthur A. Lumsdaine evaluated a number of experimental designs in family planning projects in the developing world from the methodological point of view.[4] They concluded that these experimental ef-

2. The Population Council generously shared with us the data it gathered on the progress of experiments. The unpublished appendix to the Bernard Berelson and Ronald Freedman article, "The Record of Family Planning Programs," *Studies in Family Planning*, vol. 7, no. 1 (January 1976), has been extremely useful in the preparation of this paper.

3. See the Bibliography for full references to these sources.

4. Elizabeth T. Hilton and Arthur A. Lumsdaine, "Field Trial Designs in Gauging the Impact of Fertility Planning Programs," in *Evaluation*

forts were often lacking in the methodological aspects of their design and procedure.

The studies mentioned above address some aspects of the methodological and substantive dimensions of family planning experiments. At present, however, there is no comprehensive review of the experimental efforts which analyzes both their design and the approach they tested and which evaluates their usefulness in providing guidelines for improving the services of regular family planning programs. This book attempts to fill the void. It reviews ninety-six experiments to determine the usefulness of experimental efforts in relation to the delivery of services and, on the basis of this evaluation, suggests strategies and areas for further experimentation. This study focuses on experiments which were deliberately designed to test ways to provide family planning services. Experiments were not considered if their principal objective was to test contraceptive methods or educational techniques that did not immediately lead to the acceptance or practice of family planning. Similarly excluded were experiments designed mainly to identify populations or settings most likely to produce high acceptance rates.

In reviewing these experimental efforts, this study examines the methodology used and the problems encountered, analyzes the approaches tested and the results obtained, and discusses the use that has been made of the findings and their implications for future experimentation. In the pursuit of these objectives we encountered several difficulties, however. This appraisal is the product of a desk study rather than field observation. The list of experiments reviewed, while comprehensive, is by no means exhaustive; many have simply not been publicized, and a number of those published may have eluded us. Some of the experiments have no doubt had irregularities that went unreported, but the results have been accepted without attempt-

---

and Experiment, Carl A. Bennett and Arthur A. Lumsdaine, eds. (New York: Academic Press, 1975).

ing to determine if, in fact, any irregularities existed. Not all experiments are reported as completely as we would wish; the dearth of information on cost is particularly glaring.

This work was made possible by the constant encouragement and collaboration of the director of the Development Economics Department, Ravi Gulhati, and of the chief of the Population and Human Resources Division, Timothy King. An earlier draft of this study served as the basis for a workshop held at the World Bank in May 1976. The participants in this workshop, Lee-Jay Cho, L. P. Chow, Robert J. Lapham, Ronald Ridker, John Ross, Ismail Sirageldin, and Carl Taylor as well as members of both the Population and Human Resources Division and the Population Projects Department made significant contributions to the improvement of this work.

We are indebted to the Population Council, especially to Robert J. Lapham and Roy Treadway, who made available their own compilation of materials on this topic and also provided useful comments at several stages. Ronald Freedman, Duff Gillespie, Joel Montague, Elizabeth Thompson, and John Laing also read an earlier version and contributed helpful comments.

In the early stages of this undertaking Veena Soni, a consultant for the World Bank, worked on the compilation and comparative analysis of some of the experiments in India, Taiwan, and Hong Kong.

The patient and capable secretarial assistance of Komola Ghose, Subathra Thavamoney, and Yupin Whitehead is gratefully acknowledged. Jane H. Carroll edited the final manuscript for publication.

This study would not have been possible without the cooperation of the persons previously mentioned and the supportive environment of the World Bank. We alone, of course, are responsible for any errors of omission or commission.

Roberto Cuca and Catherine S. Pierce

Part I
Analysis

CHAPTER 1

Introduction and Summary

THE EARLY ACTIVITIES OF FAMILY PLANNING ASSOCIATIONS tested the acceptability of the idea of family limitation. Later efforts addressed the suitability of particular ways to provide family planning services and attempted to improve the effectiveness and efficiency of existing programs. The record of experimentation in family planning is replete with examples of approaches that were first tried out in the experimental context and later adopted as policy. The Chulalongkorn experiment in Thailand indicated the feasibility of using previous acceptors as motivators to encourage other women to accept family planning; as a consequence, the idea was incorporated into the national program. The Shopkeeper program in Bangladesh demonstrated the effectiveness of commerical outlets in selling contraceptives; this approach is now an accepted part of the programs in Pakistan and Bangladesh and provided the basis for more recent marketing and community-based distribution programs in other countries. The Kaoshiung mass media study in Taiwan was the model for the islandwide mass communications campaign which began in 1972. The acceptability of using nonmedical personnel to prescribe pills was established through experiments. Limited undertakings of this nature prepared the way for the large-scale contraceptive inundation and distribution projects of recent years.

The experimental framework has thus proved a useful vehicle for testing new ways to offer family planning services. If an approach proves successful, it can be wholly or partially incorporated into the regular program; if not, the negative consequences are negligible. In addition to improving the performance and broadening the scope of regular programs, the experiments generated new questions that became the subject of subsequent experiments. Family planning experiments have also contributed to the development of their own methodology. Recent experiments appear to have overcome many of the methodological deficiencies that flawed earlier efforts.

Part I of this book represents a comprehensive review of ninety-six such experiments and evaluates the methodology used and the approaches tested. The usefulness of the experimental framework is discussed together with the methodological problems observed in the experiments reviewed. Also considered are the approaches that have been tested, the findings, and the implications of these findings for strategies for future experimentation. All the experiments reviewed here are described in greater detail in Part II, where references for each experiment are also given.

The Experimental Framework

From the outset, the term "experiment" has proved troublesome. It is an inaccurate label for most of these undertakings, but other possible terms (such as "innovative field studies") are cumbersome and often fall short of connoting a trial or test which the word "experiment" suggests. Thus, we have opted to use "experiment" and attach to it all the usual caveats that prevail when a concept more appropriate to the physical sciences is applied to the realm of the social sciences.[1]

The complex tasks of experimental design and measurement become even more formidable within the context of family planning. It is difficult to maintain an isolated treatment area over an extended period of time, and the presence of numerous uncontrolled variables often makes it impossible to discern the impact of the intervention on the dependent variable. When a particular approach to family planning is being tested, the dependent variable is fertility or a proxy variable such as knowledge, attitude, acceptance, or practice of family planning—all of which resist precise measurement. Changes in the dependent variable can occur as the result of a number of factors: the treatment being tested, a change in socioeconomic factors during the experiment, the delayed effect of earlier family planning efforts, the awareness that an experiment is taking place, or the effect of a survey done as a baseline for the experiment. The impact of the experimental treatment on the dependent variable is difficult to isolate from that of other forces in the experimental environment. A "true experiment" requires randomization and well-matched comparison groups. But this is difficult to achieve in a sector as complex as family planning, and quasi-experimental designs of varying measurement capabilities are a more realistic alternative.

Of the ninety-six efforts reviewed, only forty-one had control groups or alternative interventions to separate the impact of the experimental treatment from other influences on fertility; of these forty-one, twelve assigned either subjects or treatment randomly and can therefore be considered the only true experiments in terms of their design. The remaining twenty-nine must be considered quasi-experi-

1. A more detailed discussion of the term "experiment" as applied to innovative efforts in family planning services is found in Chapter 3.

ments because they lacked suitable randomization. The other fifty-five efforts, also quasi-experiments, had no control groups but simply assumed that all changes in the dependent variable were caused by the experimental treatment. Some of these experiments did not include controls because the main objective was to demonstrate the workability of the approach rather than its precise effect.

The use of controls frequently presents problems, because it is difficult to find well-matched control groups and to keep them free from contamination. Often treatment and control areas may appear to have similar properties but they differ in their exposure to a particular force. In the Danfa experiment in Ghana, for example, heavy migration made it difficult to determine the impact of the experimental intervention and certainly attenuated any comparisons that could be made with the control villages.

Although the well-designed experiment should permit precise measurement of changes in the dependent variable, changes in fertility are extremely difficult to measure. Intermediate or proxy variables therefore had to be used in most cases. In some experiments the number of acceptors was used as an indication of the impact; in others, the utilization of services was employed as a measure of success. Such indexes can be closely associated with the inputs of the experimental intervention. The vasectomy camps in India measured performance by the number of operations. Marketing schemes in Bangladesh, Sri Lanka, and Colombia used volume of sales as an indicator of achievement. The Telephone programs in Korea, Taiwan, and the Philippines considered number of calls as an index of the experiment's success. Other studies employed changes in knowledge, attitude, and practice as proxies for a decline in fertility. The relation between these proxies and fertility is, to say the least, not direct; in fact, considerable research has been devoted to clarifying this relation. The effect of an intervention on a proxy variable is thus not necessarily identical with its effect on fertility.

The measurement process may be further complicated by changing the instruments used. If the devices used in the pretest are considered inadequate, new ones may be introduced in the posttest, which will produce biased estimates of the effects. The duration of the experiment may introduce further complications. Short-run experiments may appear successful because the novelty of their approach guarantees a certain level of impact and because they satisfy the demands of a particular market. This success, however, may be short run. In contrast, experiments of long duration may be subject to interference from other factors in the experimental environment. Such phenomena as significant socioeconomic development may jeopardize the precise measurement of the effect of the intervention.

Ideally, it should be possible to replicate in a larger environment the results obtained in a limited experimental setting. Such replicability is dependent on a project's being representative and having operational validity. The experimental areas should be selected randomly to assure that they are representative of places where the approach might eventually be implemented. In most of the experiments considered here, however, the sites were not rigorously selected. Some experiments were essentially demonstration projects and representativeness was not a prime consideration; in other cases the areas were selected on pragmatic grounds such as proximity to a research institution.

The concept of operational validity includes the issues of resource requirements and acceptability of the experimental approach on a wide scale. As will be seen in Chapter 2, the concept must be applied with some flexibility according to the purpose of the project. If, indeed, the experiment is set up to test an approach that, if successful, would immediately be incorporated into a program, then it is sensible to limit its resource requirements to those that would be available in the context of the regular program. In contrast, if an experiment is mounted to demonstrate the workability of an approach, particularly in an area where there has been little previous family planning activity, the use of relatively greater resources may be justified. Furthermore, in experiments whose purpose is to determine the costs and benefits of alternative approaches, varying degrees of resource utilization may be an integral part of the experiment.

Approaches and Findings

The various family planning experiments have been grouped in six categories according to the principal approach that was tested in each. In some cases an experiment is listed under two or more headings. The six categories are:

1. Personnel: 46 experiments to determine the type and characteristics of personnel best suited for certain functions or the type of remuneration that would elicit the most effective performance.
2. Mass media: 19 experiments to determine the contribution of mass media campaigns to the effectiveness of a program.
3. Integration: 16 experiments to test whether the integration of family planning into other health programs is an effective way to provide family planning services.
4. Intensive: 10 experiments to determine whether intensive campaigns increase the acceptance and practice of family planning.
5. Incentives: 6 experiments to determine whether incentives which significantly affect the socioeconomic status of acceptors can reduce fertility.
6. Inundation: 14 experiments to determine the impact of various schemes for distributing contraceptives.

Personnel. Early family planning programs relied almost exclusively on highly trained clinical personnel, but they were in short supply almost everywhere and additional staff were needed to expand the coverage of the programs. A number of experiments paved the way for increased reliance on paramedicals and field-workers by demonstrating that they could safely be used to prescribe contraceptives. Future experiments should focus on the most effective kind of training to equip field personnel for their growing responsibilities.

Other experiments have demonstrated that personnel drawn from the same socioeconomic milieu as the target population—housewives, midwives, satisfied users—can capably provide information, stimulate motivation, and deliver contraceptive supplies. How far these experimental results can be generalized remains uncertain. It has not been proved that such field-workers are more successful than those with a superior socioeconomic status. Future experiments should try to determine the optimum mix of workers of different backgrounds in specific program situations.

Another question considered is how to pay field-workers. Results of experiments suggest that workers perform better when a bonus or incentive is offered than on an entirely time-based salary system. Payment on the basis of performance (that is, the number of acceptors recruited) is difficult to audit and costly to administer, and acceptance does not necessarily mean a commitment to practice contraception. Future experiments should explore alternative schemes which reward field-workers on the basis of nonpregnancy of the women they have recruited.

Mass media. Experiments have shown that the mass media can augment awareness and knowledge of family planning and, to a lesser extent, increase the actual practice of contraception. When combined with field-work activity such as home visits or group meetings, the use of mass media significantly increases the rate of acceptance. Future experiments should try to clarify the link between the message conveyed through media and traditional person-to-person communication.

Integrated health approach. These experiments confirm the assumption of a synergistic relation between family planning efforts and general health programs. Linking the two underscores the relation of family planning to health and at the same time facilitates the provision of services. The feasibility of this approach, however, is largely contingent on the nature of the existing health infrastructure.

Some experimental schemes have indicated a lag between improvements in health and a reduction in fertility. Other results have demonstrated the advantage of making family planning materials available right after the woman has delivered a child or had an abortion. New documentation on the link between maternal and child health care and family planning will soon be available. Questions of design and related issues of cost effectiveness of the integrated health approach are still to be resolved by future experimentation.

Intensive campaigns. Experiments were regarded as intensive in terms of the amount of inputs devoted to them as well as the comprehensiveness of the approach tested. Some efforts were in addition to a regular program; others took place without reference to an ongoing program. Results have also been mixed. Some projects have had little impact on fertility or the use of contraceptives. Others have had considerable success like the Potharam project in Thailand which convinced the Thai government to initiate a national program.

The vasectomy camps in India are perhaps another application of the intensive concept, but they were hardly experimental in the classical sense and should more correctly be considered demonstration projects. At first glance, the impact of the camps is quite spectacular, but the ethical implications and the rather low medical standards raise disturbing questions. It remains to be seen whether this concept could be applied to countries other than India.

Incentive payments to acceptors. Immediate payments to acceptors appear to increase acceptance, but the effects on continued contraceptive practice are less clear. In the Ghanaian Commodity experiment payments increased the proportion of women who actually went to a clinic after being referred there. When prompted mainly by the desire to obtain an immediate incentive, however, acceptance of a method is likely to have a low rate of continuation. An exception of course is the case of sterilization, but some ethical objections have been raised to immediate payment for irreversible sterilization. Recent experiments in India and Taiwan test the use of deferred incentives, that is, payments which are conditional on nonpregnancy, a specified number of births, or the length of birth interval, but more time is needed to measure their impact on fertility. The setting appears to be a key variable. A well-defined socioeconomic entity or a compact geographic setting (such as an island) seems to lend itself to the use of deferred incentives, whereas on a wider scale such schemes would likely prove difficult to administer. Whether the attractiveness of deferred monetary incentives will be attenuated by inflation and whether the initial motivation can be sustained are some of the questions that—it is hoped—ongoing tests and further research will clarify.

Inundation. The main objective of the inundation approach is to make contraceptives easily available to potential users by delivering them either free of charge or at subsidized prices. The approach has many variations depending on the type of contraceptive offered (usually orals and condoms) and how the client is resupplied. A number of experiments have focused on household distribution systems while others have used the mass marketing approach. The results are encouraging in that when contraceptives are made cheap and plentiful, sales have increased. But the volume of sales is hardly a reliable indicator of proper and effective use. A great deal remains to be learned about the scope and ultimate effectiveness of schemes which emphasize only the availability of contraceptives. Another issue is the optimal degree of subsidy.

Criteria for Future Experimentation

The agenda for future experimentation is already long. In addition to the six topics which past experiments have studied and which need further exploration, there are other issues which deserve attention. For example, how should abortion services complement conventional family planning efforts and how would such services affect the general level of fertility? Even broader questions need to be asked on the nature and strength of linkages between narrowly defined family planning efforts and the provision of other social and economic services such as education, social security, and insurance for children.

In selecting topics for investigation preference should be given to interventions which are not strongly affected by cultural differences and those which have the potential of bringing significant benefits. Some priority should also be given to experiments which provide needed services in the process of testing a hypothesis. Since experimentation with a single variable is often costly, a multivariate approach is preferable whenever possible. And of course both the procedures being tested and the methodology used must be feasible within the experimental framework and the environmental context.

The following categories are suggested as fruitful possibilities for future research:

1. Approaches that are already known to work but need clarification as to how and why they work. Many of the suggestions for future research proposed in the preceding section fall into this category.

2. Approaches that have some established promise. Various incentive and disincentive schemes that have been tried seem to have substantial merit, but more work remains to be done. Extending the lactation period and making abortion services available are other promising methods for re-

ducing fertility. Greater attention should also be given to modifying attitudes that affect the number of children desired through such programs as the "Stop at Two" campaign in Korea.

3. Approaches that explore the connection between socioeconomic development and fertility. Factors such as a drop in infant mortality and an increase in educational and employment opportunities for women have long been associated with a decline in fertility, but the linkages are far from clear. Integration of family planning services with the delivery of other social and economic services should be investigated in future experiments.

To take full advantage of new experimentation more attention has to focus on issues of design and measurement. Not only the content but also the methodology must be adaptable to a variety of environments, the objectives clearly stated, and the hypotheses specified. Although ideally the design should conform to the requirements of a true experiment, conditions might have to be modified for certain purposes, such as a demonstration or pilot project, where a quasi-experimental design might well suffice. The instruments and procedures for measuring the effects of the intervention should be as unobtrusive as possible and well suited to the specific variable. From the initial stages, attention should be given to the dissemination of results.

Other methodological considerations that should be addressed are the duration of the experiment and the number of hypotheses that an experiment should be designed to test. The resolution of these issues should be largely determined by the purpose of the experiment and the resources available to it.

Procedural questions must also be considered inasmuch as the relations among researchers, program managers, and policymakers may determine the success of the experimental approach. Because money and personnel for research are apt to be scarce in developing countries, they often depend on foreign resources for assistance. The motives of foreign agencies or governments involved in research are not always trusted, however. Furthermore the experimental goals of researchers may differ from the more operationally oriented goals of the program managers and policymakers who initiated the experiment, and international friction may further strain relations between them. In such a setting even the soundest and most relevant experiment would falter, and it is therefore vital to promote mutual confidence and better communication. Foreign donors and researchers should exercise restraint by not placing the interests of research above the needs of their host country and tactfully listen to the advice of local authorities who speak from familiarity with their own country and people.

CHAPTER 2

Experimental Efforts in Family Planning Programs

FAMILY PLANNING ACTIVITIES in almost every country were initiated by volunteer groups, usually doctors' or womens' organizations.[1] These early efforts were undertaken to provide a service perceived as needed rather than to affect the rate of population growth. The services were usually rendered by clinics run by the voluntary organizations, and little use was made of mass communication or motivational activities. As the demand for family planning services became more visible, the small groups of volunteers soon developed into local Family Planning Associations (FPA), which were later affiliated with the International Planned Parenthood Federation (IPPF).

The work of the Family Planning Associations in most countries can certainly be considered innovative and, in a very broad sense, experimental in nature. Their activities tested the existence of a market, the acceptability of family planning services, and the suitability of using doctors to deliver services, usually from stationary locations. Because

1. Everett M. Rogers, *Communications Strategies for Family Planning* (New York: The Free Press, 1973), pp. 10–11. In chapter 1 Rogers provides an excellent account of the evolution of family planning delivery services.

most of these undertakings were not intrinsically designed as experiments, they were not representative of the areas where they took place nor did they produce a scientific measurement of results. They were, however, definitely instrumental in the later efforts by governments. The FPAs set up the basic delivery system that governments would adopt initially and later expand.

The transition to government sponsorship of family planning services took place as the FPA clinics were absorbed by and replicated in the government's health framework. Government interest in these activities has not necessarily meant the disappearance of the FPA, but it has brought a division of functions. Typically the governments have taken over the clinical services, and the FPA have concentrated their efforts on training and communication (at least until the government has acquired the necessary expertise in these fields).

After assuming the responsibilities for providing services, the governments realized that the programs needed to improve their performance. The concepts of effectiveness, cost, and efficiency took on new importance and underscored the need for experimentation to find more effective ways of delivering services and to make more efficient use of resources. FPA, bilateral and multilateral agencies, and governments responded to this newly perceived need and initiated a series of experimental efforts.

Characteristics of the Experiments

These experimental efforts, which were undertaken to learn more about the delivery of family planning services, tested alternative delivery systems but did not usually meet the requirements of classical experimental methodology. Indeed, "true experiments" in the sense of having randomization and well-matched comparison groups are rarely encountered in this sector, and the application of the term "experiment" to these endeavors may well be questioned. Nevertheless, in this review the word "experiment" will encompass what might be most appropriately termed quasi-scientific undertakings.

Table 1 lists the experiments and identifies their experimental design, the approach tested, the year of initiation, and duration. In classifying the experiments by design the following terms were used: "Experiment" designates a true experiment having both randomization and controls. Quasi-experiments encompass four variations: "Control/test" indicates undertakings with both pretests and controls; "Control only" applies to those which lacked a pretest. Although both of these categories have controls, the absence of randomizing procedures distinguishes them from a true experiment. The term "Pretest" represents those studies in which a pretest was made but there was no control group. The category "No pretest" includes experimental undertakings with neither a pretest nor a control. A more complete discussion of the rationale underlying this classification scheme is found in Chapter 3.

In order to facilitate discussion, the approaches tested in the experiments have been reduced to six. As would be expected, some arbitrariness was involved in trying to accommodate a variety of experimental efforts in six classifications; it was felt, however, that such generalization was preferable to a multiplicity of precise but unwieldy categories. The approaches have been defined with considerable flexibility so that a number of the variations can be included under a general heading. The "Personnel" approach includes experiments which addressed what type of workers should be used as well as methods of paying workers. The classification "Mass media" includes the usual devices—radio, television, newspapers, pamphlets—and has been expanded to include experiments which used the mails and telephoning schemes as a way of reaching potential clients. The term "Integration" refers to the incorporation of family planning services with other medical care. The "Intensive"

Table 1. Characteristics of the Experiment

Country	*Experiment*	*Design*[a]	*Approach tested*[b]	*Initial year*	*Duration*[c]
Bangladesh	Comilla	No pretest	Personnel/ inundation	1961	Very long
	Dacca	Control/test	Personnel	1963	Medium
	Household Distribution	Control/test	Inundation	1975	Medium
	Shopkeeper	No pretest	Inundation	1964	Medium
Chile	Education/Postabortion	Control only	Integration	1971	Short
	San Gregorio	Pretest	Integration	1965	Medium
Colombia	Bogotá Mail/Visits	Experiment	Mass media Personnel	1973	Short
	Pamphlets	Control/test	Mass media	1972	Very short
	PRIMOPS	Pretest	Integration	1972	Very long
	PROFAMILIA Rural	No pretest	Personnel/ inundation	1970	Very long
	PROFAMILIA Urban	No pretest	Personnel/ inundation	1974	Long
	Radio	Control/test	Mass media	1969	Long
	SOMEFA	No pretest	Personnel	1974	Short
Dominican Republic	Santo Domingo	Control only	Personnel	1971	Very short
Egypt	Experimental Home Visits	No pretest	Personnel	1976	Medium
Ghana	Commodity	Control only	Incentives	1970	Very short
	Danfa	Control/test	Integration	1972	Very long
Greenland	Greenland	No pretest	Mass media	1967	Medium
Honduras	Acceptor Agents	Control only	Personnel	1972	Medium
Hong Kong	Field-workers	Experiment	Personnel	1966	Very short
	Reassurance	Experiment	Personnel	1968	Short

India	Acceptance of Orals	No pretest	Personnel	1968	Medium
	Andhra Pradesh	No pretest	Personnel	1970	Very short
	Ernakulam I	No pretest	Intensive	1970	Very short
	Ernakulam II	No pretest	Intensive	1971	Very short
	Ernakulam III	No pretest	Intensive	1972	Very short
	Gandhigram	Control/test	Integration	1962	Very long
	Gujarat	No pretest	Intensive	1971	Very short
	Hooghly	Pretest	Mass media	1966	Very short
	Khanna	Control/test	Intensive	1953	Very long
	Madras Canvasser	No pretest	Personnel	1959	Very long
	Madras Community Leaders	No pretest	Personnel	1962	Long
	Meerut	No pretest	Mass media	1966	Very short
	Mehrauli	Pretest	Integration	1963	Very long
	Multipurpose Worker	No pretest	Personnel	1970	Long
	Narangwal	Control/test	Integration	1966	Very long
	Nirodh	No pretest	Inundation	1968	Very long
	Singur	Control/test	Personnel/ mass media	1954	Very long
	Tea Estates, Assam and West Bengal	No pretest	Incentives	1965	Long
	Tea Estates (UPASI)	Pretest	Incentives	1972	Very long
Indonesia	Mojokerto	Control/test	Integration	1973	Very long
International	Community-based Distribution[d]	Pretest	Inundation	1973	Very long
	DEIDS	Pretest	Integration	1972	Very long
	Maternal, Child Health/ Family Planning	Pretest	Integration	1974	Very long
	Postpartum	No pretest	Integration	1966	Very long

(*Table continues on next page.*)

TABLE 1. *(continued)*

Country	*Experiment*	*Design*[a]	*Approach tested*[b]	*Initial year*	*Duration*[c]
Iran	Isfahan Intensive	Pretest	Intensive	1970	Medium
	Isfahan Mass Communications	Pretest	Mass media	1970	Medium
	Isfahan Model Family Planning	Pretest	Integration	1972	Long
	Isfahan Opinion Leaders	Pretest	Personnel/ mass media	1970	Short
Kenya	Kenya/Kinga	Control only	Inundation	1972	Medium
	Postpartum IUD	No pretest	Integration	1975	Medium
Korea	Cheju	Control/test	Inundation	1976	Long
	Euiryong	Control/test	Inundation	1975	Very short
	IUD Checkups	Experiment	Personnel	1967	Medium
	Koyang IUD	Pretest	Personnel	1965	Medium
	Koyang/Kimpo	Control/test	Intensive	1962	Long
	Mothers' Clubs	Experiment	Personnel	1966	Medium
	Mothers' Clubs Intensity	Experiment	Intensive	1966	Medium
	Recruitment of IUD Acceptors	No pretest	Personnel	1974	Medium
	Seoul Agents	No pretest	Personnel	1967	Medium
	Seoul Telephone	No pretest	Mass media	1972	Long
	Sungdong Gu	Control/test	Personnel/ mass media	1964	Medium

Malaysia	Bidan	No pretest	Personnel	1969	Long
Mexico	Postpartum/Postabortion	No pretest	Integration	1970	Long
	Traditional Birth Attendant	No pretest	Personnel	1974	Long
Pakistan	Lulliani	Pretest	Intensive	1961	Long
	Sialkot	Pretest	Personnel	1969	Long
Peru	Cerro de Pasco	Pretest	Personnel/ mass media	1967	Long
Philippines	Paramedical	Control/test	Personnel	1973	Short
	Telephone	No pretest	Mass media	1975	Medium
	Worker Incentives	Control/test	Personnel	1973	Medium
Puerto Rico	Communication/Content	Experiment	Mass media/ personnel	1959	Medium
Singapore	Disincentives	No pretest	Incentives	1972	Very long
Sri Lanka	Preethi	No pretest	Inundation	1973	Long
	Sweden-Ceylon	Pretest	Intensive	1958	Very long
Taiwan	Agent Incentive	Experiment	Personnel	1971	Very short
	Contraceptive Inundation	Control/test	Inundation	1974	Medium
	Educational Savings	Control/test	Incentives	1971	Very long
	Group Meetings	Experiment	Personnel	1964	Short
	IUD Free Offer	Experiment	Mass media	1964	Very short
	Kaoshiung	Pretest	Mass media	1968	Medium
	Mail-order Pills	No pretest	Mass media	1965	Very short
	Prepregnancy Health	Experiment	Personnel/ mass media	1963	Long
	Referral Fee	No pretest	Personnel	1964	Short
	Taichung	Pretest	Incentives	1974	Long
	Taipei Telephone	No pretest	Mass media	1972	Long
Thailand	Auxiliary Midwives	Experiment	Personnel	1969	Medium

(*Table continues on next page.*)

TABLE 1. *(continued)*

Country	*Experiment*	*Design*[a]	*Approach tested*[b]	*Initial year*	*Duration*[c]
	Chulalongkorn	Control/test	Personnel	1967	Short
	Potharam	No pretest	Intensive	1964	Long
	Time and Distance	No pretest	Personnel	1965	Long
	Worker Evaluation	Control	Personnel	1971	Medium
Tunisia	Political Party	Pretest	Personnel	1965	Medium
Turkey	Etimesgut	Pretest	Integration	1967	Very long
	Tarsus I	Control/test	Personnel/ inundation	1969	Short
	Tarsus II	Control/test	Personnel/ inundation	1971	Medium
Venezuela	Change Agents	Control/test	Personnel	1972	Long

Note: Each experiment is described in detail in Part II.

a. The experiments are classified by design as an "Experiment," that is, a true experiment having both controls and randomization, or as one of four types of quasi-experiments: those having both pretests and controls (Control/test); those with control groups but no pretest (Control only); those with no controls but having a pretest (Pretest); and those with neither controls nor pretest (No pretest). A more complete discussion of this classification scheme is found in Chapter 3.

b. The six approaches are categorized as experiments which addressed the questions of type of worker as well as the method of paying workers (Personnel); those which tested the incorporation of family planning services with other medical care (Integration); schemes which concentrated a variety of resources on increasing the acceptance of family planning (Intensive); those for the commercial, community, and household distribution of contraceptives (Inundation); those which used mass media; and those which used incentives.

c. Duration has been classified as: very short, 0–5 months; short, 6–11 months; medium, 12–23 months; long, 24–59 months; and very long, 5 or more years.

d. Includes schemes for community, commercial, and household distribution of contraceptives.

approach designates experiments which concentrated a variety of resources for the express purpose of increasing the number of acceptors of family planning. "Incentives" applies to rewards, either immediate or postponed, offered to acceptors of family planning services; disincentive schemes have also been included under this heading. "Inundation" refers to various methods for the distribution of contraceptives; it includes community-based programs and both commercial and household distribution schemes. The approaches are discussed at length in Chapter 4.

The regional distribution of the experiments, the period of initiation, and duration are broken down numerically in Table 2. The high concentration of experiments in certain regions of the world simply reflects the fact that the earlier a country began a family planning program, the more time it has had to grapple with the problems of the delivery system and to initiate experiments to correct those problems. Most

TABLE 2. EXPERIMENTS CLASSIFIED BY LOCALE, PERIOD OF INITIATION, AND DURATION

		Period of initiation			*Duration*		
Country or region	*Experiments reviewed*	*Before 1965*	*1965–69*	*After 1969*	*Less than one year*	*One to two years*	*More than two years*
India	19	6	6	7	7	1	11
Taiwan	11	4	2	5	5	2	4
Korea	11	2	5	4	1	7	3
Rest of Asia	28	6	9	13	6	10	12
Latin America	16	1	3	12	5	3	8
Africa	6	0	1	5	1	4	1
Greenland	1	0	1	0	0	1	0
International	4	0	1	3	0	0	4
Total	96	19	28	49	25	28	43

Source: Appendix A.

of the experiments considered have taken place in Asia (nineteen in India, eleven in Taiwan, eleven in Korea, and twenty-eight elsewhere in Asia). Only sixteen of the experiments were in Latin American countries, one in Greenland, and six in African countries. Four of the experiments were designed to cover several countries and are classified as international.

The number of experimental efforts has increased with time as more countries have adopted official family planning programs. Only nineteen of the ninety-six experiments considered were begun before 1965; twenty-eight were initiated between 1965 and 1969, and forty-nine have been undertaken since 1970.

The duration of the experiments varies and is related to the design as well as to the approach being tested. Twenty-five of the experiments took less than a year; twenty-eight took between one and two years; and forty-three have taken, or are expected to take, more than two years. With the exception of the experiments in India and the international experiments, there has been a tendency in all the regions for experiments to last less than two years. As can be observed from Table 1, most true experiments had a relatively short duration.

Contraceptive Methods Used

Although experimentation with contraceptives is not considered here as such, the success of any delivery system and the results of any experiment depend, at least partially, on the kinds of contraceptives offered. Table 3 shows the contraceptive methods used in these experiments and divides them according to the period when the experiments were initiated. Developments in contraceptive technology and the acceptance of new methods over time are thus revealed.

In the early undertakings neither the IUD (intrauterine de-

TABLE 3. CONTRACEPTIVES USED IN THE EXPERIMENTS AND PERIOD OF INITIATION

Period of initiation	*Number of experiments*	*Rhythm and coitus interruptus*	*Diaphragm*	*Condom*	*Pill*	*IUD*	*Sterilization*	*Unclear or unknown*
1950–59	5	1	4	3	0	0	2	1
1960–64	14	2	4	6	0	8	6	5
1965–69	28	2	2	4	8	19	3	4
1970–75	44	2	4	14	17	15	7	15
1975–79	5	0	0	2	4	3	2	0
Total	96[a]	7	14	29	29	45	20	25

a. The sum of the components is larger than the total because multiple methods were offered in several experiments.

vice) nor the pill was offered. These methods were considered too new even for an experimental setting, and more traditional and conventional techniques were thought to stand a better chance of being accepted. The IUD was first introduced in the 1960–64 period; it was the predominant method used during the years 1965 to 1969 and continued to be an important device in the experiments of the 1970–74 period. The pill gained acceptance more slowly, but it has become the most widely offered method in the most recent experiments. Improvements in its chemical composition have persuaded governments to liberalize its use, and bulk buying by donor agencies, especially USAID (United States Agency for International Development), has increased its availability at lower prices. The latest innovation in contraceptive technology, the injectable, has been used in only one of the experiments reviewed. It can be expected to follow a course similar to that of the IUD and the pill and will probably be offered with greater frequency as more becomes known about it.

Of the conventional methods, the condom has been offered consistently over the years and has in fact experienced increased usage in recent years. As community-based distribution schemes become more widespread, the condom will certainly be used more extensively in the future. The use of sterilization has been concentrated mainly in the Indian subcontinent. Experiments have usually focused on male rather than female sterilization. Experiments for which information on the precise methods offered was not available have been listed in the last column. While the date and the area of the experiment would permit reasonably accurate assumptions regarding the methods, we have refrained from making such assumptions.

CHAPTER 3

Methodological Problems Encountered

EXPERIMENTAL EFFORTS IN FAMILY PLANNING have been used to determine, on a limited basis, whether the particular approach being tested is effective and, if so, whether it can be used in a regular program. At first glance, experimentation appears to be an ideal vehicle for such research. The investigator is able to manipulate the intensity and duration of stimuli and to observe the effects on other variables. The strength of this type of research is, however, largely contingent on the quality of the experimental design. It should permit measurement of the effects of the experiment and replication of the results. These two topics will be the focus of this chapter.

Measurement of Experimental Effects

The theoretical issues encountered in designing any experiment are especially thorny when dealing with experiments in family planning. It is difficult to isolate the area geographically and almost impossible to control many of the extraneous variables. Particularly problematic are the issues of experimental design, measurement of the dependent variable, and the duration of the experiment.

THEORETICAL DESIGN

The goal in experimental research is to determine, as precisely as possible, the effects of the experimental stimuli. A design with strong internal validity is therefore essential to answer the basic questions: Did the intervention account for the change in the dependent variable? Have all plausible competing hypotheses other than the experimental treatment been ruled out? Strong internal validity reduces the ambiguity in interpreting the results of the experiment. Campbell and Stanley list eight classes of extraneous variables which might confound the effects of the experimental treatment if not controlled for in the experimental design.[1]

Since most of the experimental studies considered did not meet the requirements for total internal validity, they cannot be called true experiments; they can, however, be accommodated within the Campbell-Stanley classification of quasi-experiments. A true experiment requires a design in which the effect of the experimental stimuli or intervention on the dependent variable can be isolated from that of other factors. In testing a particular system for the delivery of family planning services, the dependent variable is fertility or some other intermediate or proxy variable such as knowledge, attitude, acceptance, or practice of family planning. A change in the dependent variable during the experiment can be caused by the delivery system being tested, by changes in socioeconomic factors, by the delayed effect of earlier family planning efforts, by the knowledge that an experiment was taking place, or even by the effect of a survey done as a baseline for the experiment. These different rea-

1. Donald J. Campbell and Julian C. Stanley, *Experimental and Quasi-Experimental Designs for Research* (Chicago: Rand McNally College Publishing Co., 1963), p. 5. Variables which threaten internal validity represent the effects of history, maturation, testing, instrumentation, statistical regression, selection biases, experimental mortality, and selection-maturation interaction.

sons for change in the dependent variable can be summarized with the Ross-Smith equation,[2]

$$d = P + E + U + I_{PE} + I_{PU} + I_{EU} + I_{PEU}$$

in which d is the difference observed in the dependent variable after it was subjected to the experimental treatment. E, P, and U, each operating alone, represent the effects of the experimental stimulus, of a pretest, and of uncontrolled events, respectively. The other terms in the equation represent the interactions among the three principal variables.

There is no simple design in which the value of E can clearly and unmistakenly be determined, but some designs are better than others because they reduce the number of terms in the equation that have to be ignored or assumed. Campbell and Stanley maintain that the basic design for a true experiment must consist of at least two groups, one which receives the experimental stimulus and the other which does not. The groups have to be equivalent, which implies that the individuals are assigned randomly to each group. Because of this equivalency no pretest is necessary; therefore the terms P, I_{PE}, I_{PU}, and I_{PEU} in the equation can be ignored, and only the term I_{EU} has to be given an assumed value. This design leaves open the question of whether the dependent variable was equal for the two groups before the intervention. The only possible error in this case is the sampling error that comes with randomization; statistical analysis, however, can provide estimates of the error in that assumption.

The optimum experimental design is the Solomon Four-Group design in which four equivalent groups are chosen.[3] Two of the groups receive the experimental intervention but only one of the two receives the pretest. In the other

2. John Ross and Perry Smith, "Orthodox Experimental Designs," in *Methodology in Social Research*, H. M. Blalock and A. B. Blalock, eds. (New York: McGraw-Hill, 1968), pp. 333–89.

3. Campbell and Stanley, *Experimental and Quasi-Experimental Designs*, pp. 24–25.

two groups only one is subjected to the pretest but neither receives the experimental intervention. In this design three of the terms in the equation have to be assumed and none are ignored. This design permits the effects of the pretest to be observed. The pretest itself clarifies the status of the dependent variable prior to the experiment, and the large number of groups increases the statistical confidence of the experiment.

DESIGN PROBLEMS IN FAMILY PLANNING EXPERIMENTS

Some idea of the quality of the experimental designs encountered in the field studies reviewed can be seen in Table 4. The studies have been divided into five categories of design ranging from the most rigorous to those with neither a pretest nor a control. Under the heading "true experiments" are those efforts for which control groups or similar comparison groups existed and in which subjects were assigned randomly to either the experimental or the control group.[4] Studies listed in columns 2 and 3 employed control groups but cannot be considered true experiments because there was neither randomization of subjects nor random assignment of treatment. If pretests were done for either the experimental or control groups or both, then the study was entered in column 2; cases with control groups but no pretest of either group are found in column 3. Items listed in columns 4 and 5 are those in which no controls were used. Table 4 also indicates the duration of the experiment since this information is relevant to the design.

Table 4 indicates that only 41 of the 96 field studies had a control group, even though the definition of control group was extended to include alternative interventions. This broad interpretation was based on the assumption that the

4. In some cases it was the intervention that was assigned randomly to one of the groups being studied, but we have taken this to fulfill the requirement of randomization.

researchers wanted to find out which of several interventions was the best. From the beginning they probably expected that at least one of the interventions would have an effect of a certain order of magnitude; one of the alternate treatments could therefore function as a control group and permit the comparative measurement of the other interventions. Randomization, rather than the existence of a control group, determines whether a field study can be classified as a true experiment. In most of the cases that had control groups, subjects were not assigned randomly, and thus the experimental and control groups were not equivalent. Even if some kind of matching were attempted, it could not be assumed that uncontrolled variables would affect the two groups in the same way.

Although control groups are often thought to strengthen the findings of an experiment, they are not without drawbacks. In some cases the control and experimental areas were not effectively isolated; contamination occurred and made it impossible to measure the effect of the experimental intervention. An example of this problem is found in the Mothers' Clubs Intensity experiment (Korea), where some of the inputs for the experimental program made their way into the control areas. In other instances either the experimental or the control area can be affected by alternate programs. In the Koyang/Kimpo study (Korea), the control area, Kimpo, began receiving official family planning services while the experiment was taking place; this study, which was intended to measure the effect of E, could therefore measure only the difference between E and the impact of the government intervention. Another limitation is that the existence of one experimental area and one control area is essentially equivalent to one observation for each cell with the consequent effect on the number of degrees of freedom. A design having multiple experimental and control areas, as in the Prepregnancy Health study in Taiwan, offers a possible solution for this problem.

Treatment and control areas which appear to have simi-

TABLE 4. EXPERIMENTS CLASSIFIED BY DESIGN AND DURATION

Duration	*True experiments (randomization and controls)* (1)	*Quasi-experiments*			
		Control/test (2)	*Control only* (3)	*Pretest* (4)	*No pretest* (5)
0–5 months	Group Meetings Agent Incentive Field-workers IUD Free Offer	Euiryong Pamphlets	Commodity Santo Domingo	Hooghly	Mail-order Pills Meerut Andhra Pradesh Ernakulam I Ernakulam II Ernakulam III Gujarat SOMEFA
6–14 months	Reassurance Bogotá Mail/Visits	Chulalongkorn Tarsus I Paramedical	Education/post-abortion	Isfahan Opinion Leaders	Referral Fee
1 year	Mothers' Clubs Mothers' Clubs Intensity IUD Checkups	Dacca Sungdong Gu Worker Incentives Tarsus II	Kenya/Kinga Acceptor Agents Worker Evaluation	Koyang IUD San Gregorio Kaoshiung Political Party	Acceptance of Orals Seoul Agents Experimental Home Visits

	Communication/ Content Auxiliary Midwives	Contraceptive Inundation Household Distribution		Isfahan Intensive Isfahan Mass Communications	Greenland Recruitment of IUD Acceptors Postpartum IUD Philippines Telephone Shopkeeper
2–4 years	Prepregnancy Health	Koyang/Kimpo Change Agents Radio Cheju		Taichung Lulliani Cerro de Pasco Isfahan Model Family Planning Sialkot	Multipurpose Worker Madras Community Leaders Tea Estates, Assam and West Bengal Bidan Potharam PROFAMILIA Urban Postpartum/postabortion Traditional Birth Attendant Seoul Telephone Taipei Telephone Time and Distance[a]

(*Table continues on next page.*)

TABLE 4. *(continued)*

Duration	*True experiments (randomization and controls)* (1)	*Quasi-experiments*			
		Control/test (2)	*Control only* (3)	*Pretest* (4)	*No pretest* (5)
5 or more years		Khanna Narangwal Singur Danfa Gandhigram Educational Savings Mojokerto		Sweden-Ceylon DEIDS[b] Mehrauli Etimesgut Tea Estates (UPASI) Maternal, Child Health/Family Planning[b] Community-based Distribution[b] PRIMOPS	Comilla Postpartum[b] Madras Canvasser Nirodh Preethi PROFAMILIA Rural Disincentives[a]

Source: Table 1.

a. These quasi-experiments might be more accurately termed post hoc studies.

b. Experiments undertaken on an international basis. In some instances pretest data does exist, in others it does not. Postpartum has been listed in column 5, because pretests were usually not part of this intervention. Community-based distribution also includes commercial and household distribution of contraceptives.

lar properties are frequently exposed to different forces. The experimental villages in the Danfa (Ghana) experiment, for example, were subject to heavy migration which interfered considerably with the experimental intervention. The lack of comparability between the treatment and control areas in this case was owing to inappropriate selection of the areas rather than the more usual problem of contamination of the control group.

Furthermore, comparability decreases with the passage of time. The longer the time span the greater the likelihood that other factors will intrude. By using a control group, the researcher hopes not only to measure change but also to be able to ascribe that change to specific isolated factors with some confidence. As the duration of the experiment lengthens, however, there is increased risk that the control area will be affected by a set of socioeconomic forces different from those at work in the treatment area. Thus, a difference in the dependent variable in the two areas could no longer be attributed simply to the experiment. In such cases the advantage of having controls is greatly diminished.

Table 4 also lists studies which did not use control groups or alternative interventions. Since these interventions were planned and controlled by the researcher, the lack of a control group can be seen as a defect in design. In some cases the rest of the country was assumed to be the control, but this would be valid only if the experimental group had been randomly chosen from the whole population. The studies shown in column 4 had both pre- and posttests but assumed that all the changes in the dependent variable were due to the intervention, E. The experimental design of these quasi-experiments simply assigned a value of zero to the pretest and to the interaction of the pretest with the experimental variable. Uncontrolled variables were ignored as were their interactive effects with either the stimulus or the pretest. The studies in column 5 ignored all other factors except E. In addition, those studies could not measure precisely changes in the dependent variable in the absence of a pretest.

Among the reasons cited for not including control groups was the assumption that other factors would not affect fertility behavior during the intervention. In experiments of short duration such an assumption might be valid; where the intervention took place over an extended period, this assumption has to be rejected. In some instances control groups were not used because the specific aim was not to test whether the intervention would have a specific effect on the dependent variable, but rather to show program managers that the approach was generally effective and should be adopted for the regular family planning program. Another group of cases which assumed from the beginning that the approach was effective were in essence pilot projects. They attempted to improve the approach in question before it was expanded to the regular program.

MEASURING THE DEPENDENT VARIABLE

The ultimate objective of a family planning delivery system is to reduce fertility, but for an intervention to begin to affect fertility a period of at least two years is required. Since most family planning experiments are short run, usually lasting less than two years, intermediate or proxy variables have to be used as the dependent variable.

THE PRECISION OF MEASUREMENT INDEXES

The most widely used intermediate variables indicate the extent to which services are used, such as number of acceptors or number of clinic visits. The success of the intervention is thus measured by outputs that can be closely associated with the inputs of the intervention. The Ernakulam and Gujarat vasectomy camps in India measured performance by the number of operations performed. The Shopkeeper program (Bangladesh) and marketing schemes such as Nirodh (India), Preethi (Sri Lanka), and PROFAMILIA (Colombia) used volume of sales as an indicator of achievement. The telephone programs in Korea, Taiwan, and the Philippines considered number of calls as an index of the experiment's success. Other studies such as the Kaoshiung (Taiwan) project employed changes in knowledge, attitude, and practice as proxies for a decline in fertility. The relation between these proxies and fertility is, to say the least, not direct; in fact, considerable research has been devoted to clarifying this relation. The effect of an intervention on a proxy variable is not necessarily identical with the effect on fertility itself.

Measuring the changes in the dependent variable may also be complicated by the use of different measuring instruments. Those used in the pretest may not be considered adequate for the posttest, but if a new and improved instrument is introduced it may produce biased estimates of the different effects. This could possibly have occurred in the Narangwal (India) experiment where there was constant concern about improving the measuring instruments.

THE DURATION OF THE EXPERIMENT

The duration of an experiment is another factor that affects measurement. In short-run experiments the impact effect and the partial market effect may distort the results. The impact effect is a variation of the Hawthorne effect, that is, change occurs in the objective variable simply because the intervention takes place, and not because the approach being tested is in any way effective.[5] The impact effect is obvious in the case of advertising campaigns, which—regardless of their form or content—have an impact on the target

5. Fred N. Kerlinger, *Foundations of Behavioral Research*, 2d ed. (New York: Holt, Rinehart, and Winston, 1973), p. 345. Since all experiments, regardless of duration, are subject to the Hawthorne effect, measurement should be as unobtrusive as possible.

population because of their novelty. Thus, the results are attributable more to the fact of experimentation than to the intervention.

The second difficulty with short-term results, the partial market effect, arises because the general market for family planning includes diverse groups of people. Some will accept family planning services only if offered in a particular way; an experiment using this desired approach may obtain very good results in the short run but may soon saturate the partial market. Because of its brief duration, however, the experiment may not reveal any evidence of saturation. Its misleading conclusions are unmasked only when the approach is given wider use in a more general program and the effects of market saturation become apparent.

The notion of a composite of small, heterogeneous markets for family planning services appears to be validated by the program in Taiwan. The policy there has been simply to add to the ongoing program new approaches that have proved successful as short-term experiments. It could be argued that adding layers of services, rather than replacing the old with the new, has kept the Taiwanese program sensitive to the multiple markets that must be reached.

The impact and partial market effects should not be used to discredit the small short-run experiment. As with advertising campaigns, an approach can be tried until its impact is blunted and then it can be replaced. In addition, small short-run experiments are useful for testing low-cost operational approaches that do not require important policy changes. In this case adoption of an approach on the basis of its performance in a short-run experiment should be examined from a financial point of view. If it would be very costly to adopt and subsequently to discard the approach, it should be subjected to a longer period of experimentation before being put to general use.

Experiments of long duration pose their own set of measurement problems regardless of the quality of the initial design. High rates of immigration or emigration, either permanent or transitory, jeopardize measurement procedures, as was observed in the Danfa (Ghana) experiment. Major changes in the socioeconomic environment may also reduce the possibility of determining accurately the effect of an intervention.

Replicability

The principal objective of experimentation is to test an approach on a representative sample of a given population to determine whether that approach can be successfully implemented in a larger setting. The ability to generalize results depends on the external validity or representativeness of the experimental design. Has the population studied been randomly selected? Were there controls for the reactive effects of testing and the interactive effects of selection biases and the experimental variable?[6] Replicability is also contingent on operational validity, that is, use of resources in the experiment must be replicable within a regular program, and the approach and sponsorship must be acceptable in a broader context.

REPRESENTATIVENESS

For the most part, the efforts considered were deficient in terms of external validity. No rigorous procedures were followed in choosing experimental areas or target populations, but a conscientious effort was usually made to select areas that would be representative of the places where the expanded approach might eventually be implemented. This provided some assurance that the results of the experiment could be generalized. As far as can be discerned, in only one of the experiments considered (Auxiliary Midwives, Thai-

6. See Campbell and Stanley, *Experimental and Quasi-Experimental Designs*, pp. 5 and 6, for other factors threatening external validity.

land) was a country first divided into sections and then the experimental and control areas selected at random.

There are two basic reasons for the lack of rigor in selecting experimental areas. First, some of the experiments were set up as demonstration or pilot projects or as innovative approaches added to the regular program. They were not intended to be experiments in the classical sense and therefore made no pretense of being representative. Examples of this type are the Ernakulam and Gujarat vasectomy camps in India, the retrospective studies of workers in the Madras Canvasser (India) and Bidan (Malaysia) experiments; the Time and Distance study in Thailand; the marketing studies of Nirodh (India) and Preethi (Sri Lanka); and the communications studies using radio in Colombia and the telephone in Taiwan, Korea, and the Philippines.

Second, even in those cases that were specifically undertaken as experiments it was necessary to consider factors of convenience. They had to be conducted in places accessible to the researchers so that the intervention could be easily controlled and measured; this was especially necessary in experiments of long duration. The cost of running an experiment often made it impractical to test an approach in widely dispersed places. The Singur study (India) and the studies at Comilla (Bangladesh) are examples where proximity to a research center partly determined the site of the experiment. In many instances, such as Santo Domingo and some of the Taiwan endeavors, the experiments were carried out in a major city or its environs.

OPERATIONAL VALIDITY

Before an experiment is initiated, certain basic conditions should be established. The ultimate goal of any experimental effort is that, if successful, it will be adopted and expanded by the government. Therefore, it is imperative that the resources used in the experiment be realistic in terms of what would be available, proportionately, for a project under government auspices. In addition, it is only sensible that the approach being tested be politically and socially acceptable.

Resource requirements. Under this heading of resources two issues should be considered: the appropriate level of resource utilization for an experiment and the assumptions that can be made both about the availability of resources and about the amount of time necessary to expand an intervention from a limited experimental setting to a national program.

The level of resources that should be used is closely related to the purposes of the undertaking. If an experiment is mounted for the purpose of incorporating the approach (if it proves successful) into the regular program with as little modification as possible, then it is prudent to use resources on a scale that would be available within the regular program. Management, clinical and motivational personnel, physical facilities, and, of course, funds are essential for the delivery of family planning services, but these resources are usually scarce in developing countries. Consequently, many experiments are designed either to reduce total costs or to redefine tasks in a way that makes less intensive use of particularly scarce resources.

Some experiments have employed resources that simply could not be duplicated within a regular program. The Sialkot project in Pakistan used motivational workers of an exceptionally high quality. Once the approach was extended to the whole country, it was impossible to find workers of a similar caliber at local levels.

Staff supervision is a major factor in determining whether experimental results are likely to be replicable on a wide scale. Supervision is likely to be much better in an experiment than in a regular program. The small scale of most experiments makes it easy to organize the staff and to ensure that they are given clear priorities and work programs. In addition, those in charge may communicate their enthusiasm and desire for success to the whole staff, thus providing an incentive for work that is absent from a regular government program. The Gandhigram experiment (India) achieved a somewhat controversial success by doubling the density of certain workers. The high levels of training and supervision may have been made possible by the proximity of the area to the institute. In any case, the success of the program in a larger area, added later to the experiment, has been less striking. In judging replicability, therefore, the size of the experiment as measured by the total expenditure, the number of staff members, or the target population may well be crucial. Administrative problems which might remain hidden in a small-scale effort are more likely to surface in large undertakings.

Some experiments may be too expensive to have any realistic hope of adoption. In Narangwal (India) the results suggest that when family planning is combined with health and nutrition services for mothers and children there is less cost for each new acceptor than with other service packages tested. The total cost per capita was, of course, higher for the combined services, but there were the additional benefits of improved health and nutrition. This higher cost of combined services could prove to be beyond the budgetary resources of a government if such a plan were adopted for the whole country.

Most of the experiments were undertaken as exercises that could lead to modification of an ongoing program. In some cases, however, where there was no regular program and relatively little family planning activity, the experiment was initiated to demonstrate the acceptability of the idea and the feasibility of the approach. In these circumstances substantially greater resources would be needed than would be available for a regular program. Thus the experiment itself may be costly even though the approach being tested is not inherently expensive nor beyond the reach of a regular program.

Other experiments are mounted in an effort to determine the costs and benefits of alternative approaches. The amount and kinds of resources used may be varied to determine the effect on family planning of different total expenditures as well as of alternative ways of allocating a fixed budget. Such experiments might provide the basis for estimating the budgetary and training resources needed to expand an intervention from a limited experimental setting to a national program in varying amounts of time. Viewed in a different way, such experiments indicate the resources necessary to achieve different levels of family planning practice or of fertility.

Acceptability of the experiment. One condition for replicability is that no social, ethical, or political barriers block adoption of the experimental approach on a wider scale. Social acceptability has been tested by a number of experiments before undertaking a national program. In none of the experiments considered did the new approaches provoke so much opposition that they had to be discontinued. It is likely, however, that such conflict was simply not reported, and thus no record exists of experiments discontinued for this reason. In some experiments, however, religious, political, and other types of opposition have had to be overcome by the researchers. In the Isfahan Intensive project (Iran), women resented being interviewed, frequently and extensively, on personal matters by young unmarried female health officers in spite of the fact that the interviewers enjoyed some status in the community. The Madras Canvasser program (India) elicited hostile responses because of the overaggressiveness of the recruiters. The relatively little opposition encountered in most of the experiments may be attributed to the careful choice of location. Especially when the intervention was intended as a demonstration rather than as an experiment, the location was selected in such a way that the success of the treatment was assured. The Madras Community Leaders demonstration program (India) is an explicit example of this selective process; the villages chosen were relatively free from friction and had no religious objections to family planning.

The acceptability of an approach to the society in general is no guarantee that the experiment, if successful, will be replicated. The government's attitude toward the experiment and its participation in it may be of greater importance. Experiments should therefore be coordinated with the national family planning program.

The nature of the sponsoring institution—whether government, family planning association, or another private agency—may influence the eventual acceptance by the government. Responsibility for experiments carried out by the government itself might be assigned to a government agency, the family planning organization, the Ministry of Health, or a semiautonomous institution charged with research in family planning. Most of the experiments in the Indian subcontinent, in Isfahan (Iran), and in the Philippines have been under government auspices. Such sponsorship implies that the government has a practical interest in the results of the experiments and is seeking to modify its own delivery system rather than simply to increase knowledge in the area of family planning.[7] One drawback of experiments carried out under government auspices is that the program may become a demonstration or pilot project with a commitment to obtain positive results at any price. Another problem is allocation of costs. The real costs of the experiment may be difficult to separate from the cost of regular program activities or even of other associated activities (health, for example) of the government.

Experiments in Puerto Rico, Colombia, Mexico, and Hong Kong have for the most part been sponsored by local Family Planning Associations (FPA); in Taiwan many government-sponsored experiments used the FPA as an execut-

7. If one branch of the government is interested in an experiment but another branch is not, the usefulness of the experiment may be diminished. The four experiments in Isfahan (Iran) offer an example of this problem.

ing agency. Because of the scarcity of resources, experiments carried out by the local FPA tended to be simpler and of shorter duration than those funded by governments. Although there are some exceptions, national FPA are usually limited in their capacity for research and evaluation. Their experiments are geared primarily to the delivery of services and are therefore often deficient in design and measurement. The FPA were, however, willing to take risks and began experimenting in family planning long before governments or other institutions were willing to mount such efforts. In many cases FPA programs can be considered totally experimental.

The third group of sponsors has been universities (Chulalongkorn in Thailand, Yonsei in Korea, and San Gregorio in Chile) and other private groups, often with aid from foreign universities and foundations. As would be expected, the experiments conducted under university auspices tend to be better designed and measured because of the research capacity of the sponsor.

One of the principal problems with experiments conducted by the FPA or by private groups is that they may not enjoy the full cooperation of the government or other organizations. Consequently, during the implementation of the experimental intervention, competing action programs by other institutions may impede the proper measurement of the results. Unfortunately, even collaboration with or sponsorship by the government does not necessarily prevent this problem. In the cases of Koyang/Kimpo (Korea) and Santo Domingo (Dominican Republic) regular programs were extended to the control areas thus reducing both the usefulness of those controls and the validity of the experimental results.

Some experiments are executed by a combination of the three types of agencies and enjoy, to some extent, the advantages of them all—collaboration with government, the endorsement of an FPA, the research capabilities of universities, and funding and technical assistance from foreign groups. At the same time, this multiple sponsorship may prove troublesome, especially when foreign governments are involved. An example of this is the Narangwal project (India) which suffered from the deterioration in relations between the Indian and the U.S. governments after the India-Pakistan war in 1971.

CHAPTER 4

Approaches and Findings

ALL THE EXPERIMENTS under discussion tested various approaches to the delivery of family planning services. The objective was to discover ways to increase the acceptance and practice of family planning and thus eventually to reduce fertility. The different schemes tested do not lend themselves to neat categorizations, but an attempt has been made to place each experiment in one of six possible categories according to the declared (or assumed) principal approach tested. (The six categories are defined in the Introduction.) In cases where a single category was plainly inadequate the experiment is listed under two or more headings. The number of experiments in each category of approach and in each period of initiation appears in Table 5, and this classification forms the basis for the discussion in this chapter.

Personnel

As can be seen from Table 5 a considerable number of experiments have addressed the question of what type of personnel should be used to motivate and recruit acceptors and to deliver family planning services. Early family plan-

Table 5. Experiments Classified According to Approach Tested and Period of Initiation

		Personnel							
		Type							
Period of initiation	*Number of experiments*	*Motivational*	*Clinical*	*Payment*	*Mass media*	*Integration*	*Intensive*	*Incentives*	*Inundation*
1950–59	5	3	0	0	2	0	2	0	0
1960–64	14	6	0	1	3	2	3	0	2
1965–69	28	15	1	0	7	5	0	1	2
1970–74	44	15	1	3	6	9	5	5	7
1975–79	5	1	0	0	1	0	0	0	3
Total[a]	96	40	2	4	19	16	10	6	14

Source: Appendix B.

a. The addition of components exceeds the total because multiple approaches were employed in many experiments.

ning programs relied almost exclusively on clinical personnel. This emphasis shifted because physicians were in short supply, it was realized that a more aggressive system was needed both to stimulate demand and to deliver services, and there was a need to reach outlying areas. Since the role of physicians within the context of family planning is fairly well defined, most experiments focused on expanding the functions of paraprofessionals. Of the two experiments that addressed the use of clinical personnel, one tested whether there was a preference for male or female physicians to insert IUDs and whether it would be acceptable for nurses to perform this task. The sex of the inserters was shown to be inconsequential and nurses were accepted (Koyang IUD, Korea).

Paraprofessionals have been used increasingly to insert IUDs and to prescribe oral contraceptives. They usually receive some training which enables them to perform a simple pelvic examination and to evaluate whether a woman's medical history contraindicates the use of the pill. The initial concern in using paramedicals was the question of safety. The Auxiliary Midwife experiment (Thailand) addressed this issue and found that during the first year (1969) of prescription of orals by auxiliary midwives there was no increase in the incidence of side effects or complications. Largely as a result of this study, the Ministry of Public Health ruled in 1970 that all auxiliary midwives who had received the basic family planning training course could prescribe the pill. The Danfa project in Ghana introduced the home insertion of IUDs by nurse midwives, and as of 1974 midwives in Korea were also permitted to insert IUDs.

The success of these and similar experiments paved the way for expanding the role of paramedical personnel and for using other trained lay workers as well to prescribe orals. In Sialkot (Pakistan) field-workers dispensed pills, and in the Pamphlets experiment (Colombia) pharmacists prescribed pills. Suitable and thorough training should enhance the effectiveness and acceptability of such paraprofessionals.

Perhaps future research should address the specifics of curriculum and length of training period needed to equip paraprofessionals to function more efficiently.

Once it was recognized that an "outreach" system was an effective way to meet existing demand and to generate new demand, the issue then became what kind of field-workers would work most effectively. The function of outreach workers was to provide information, stimulate motivation, and either provide contraceptives or refer potential acceptors to clinics. Would workers with social and economic background similar to that of their clients be more successful in broaching this sensitive topic of family planning, or would clients respond more readily to those whom they perceived as superior and therefore more competent in the complexities of contraception?[1] Was the sex of the field-worker an important factor in reaching the widest possible audience and in conforming to the cultural norms of a particular setting?

Unfortunately, the classification by sex and socioeconomic status of the worker sheds little light on which is the most effective combination. Participation of both sexes was usually found in experiments such as the Madras Community Leaders and Multipurpose Worker in India as well as those which used local people to distribute contraceptives. In most instances when workers of only one sex were employed, they addressed members of their own sex. Most of the single sex experiments featured communication among females; in the Madras Canvasser (India), the only exception, male workers sought out male clients.

1. Everett M. Rogers provides a useful discussion of the homophily and heterophily principle as it operates in the relation between the change agent and the client. The homophilous source is viewed by a client as having "safety credibility"; the heterophilous source possesses "competence credibility." Rogers concludes that both are necessary at different stages of the recruitment process. During the persuasion stage safety credibility predominates; at the decisionmaking stage competence credibility assumes greater importance. (*Communications Strategies for Family Planning* [New York: The Free Press, 1973], pp. 400–01.)

The results of these experiments also leave open the question of whether workers are more effective when their socioeconomic status is similar or superior to that of the client population. The argument for the use of each type is persuasive. On the one hand, it is felt that the sensitivity and hesitance of people unfamiliar with the practice of family planning are best overcome by workers whose background is similar to theirs. If the potential client is able to identify with the change agent, his or her apprehensiveness is diminished. On the other hand, because the practice of family planning is often perceived as alien and complex, well-trained personnel and community leaders are often considered the more desirable agents. Their endorsement lends legitimacy to a concept sometimes regarded as suspect; their skill and competence allays the doubt and the ignorance connected with techniques of family planning.

Although it is not our intention to discuss each of these experiments, we are impressed by the simplicity and effectiveness of many which used available personnel, that is, workers from the same background as the target population. In the Seoul Agents experiment (Korea) various local people were paid a fee to recruit IUD acceptors. The agents included housewives, the leaders of a neighborhood subdivision, midwives, beauty salon operators, and even a woman church deacon. According to the results, all the agents performed well.[2] The Thailand Time and Distance study is another example of a relatively simple undertaking that increased the demand for family planning services. It demonstrated that word-of-mouth communication was an extremely effective method of recruiting new acceptors. In any experiment there is a close relation between personnel and the patterns of communication in the community. Agents with attributes similar to the target audience are

2. Possible confounding effects should be pointed out. The experiment took place against the background of publicity in the mass media for the national program. The workers received an incentive, and physicians were readily available to insert IUDs.

able to take advantage of the existing network of natural communication, and community leaders enlisted as agents cannot only tap this same network but also add to it the dimension of authority which flows from their status and role.

The record on the relative merits of homophilous and heterophilous workers is inconclusive. Experiments using each type have met with success, but the few that compare them have not provided clear answers. The lack of a strong indicator in favor of one type of worker or the other raises the broader and perhaps more significant question of how much can be generalized from the results of an experiment. The successful use of a certain type of change agent may be a function of the setting, the stage of development that family planning has reached in the area, or the scope of the experiment. In view of the situation-specific variables of each experiment and program, it would be foolhardy to embrace either approach to the exclusion of the other. The very inconclusiveness of these experiments with different types of personnel might well be instructive for managers of family planning programs. It suggests that both types of change agents could fulfill needed and complementary functions and makes it incumbent on the program manager to assess which would be better. An obvious conclusion is that more experimentation should be done to determine the optimum mix of workers of different backgrounds in given social and economic environments or for the different segments in the family planning market.

In addition to selecting the type of field-worker needed at a particular stage in the development of a family planning program, there is also the question of the best way to pay the workers in order to guarantee optimum performance. Should they be paid a regular salary only, or salary plus bonuses for meeting a certain quota, or should they be compensated for each acceptor recruited? Since this issue confronts every regular program, a number of experiments have been mounted to find the best solution. The Taiwan Referral Fee and Philippine Worker Incentives studies indicate that payment for each acceptor works well. In the Taiwan case lay motivators were used to recruit acceptors. At the end of six months the number of their recruitments equaled that of a good field-worker, but because lay motivators were paid by the case the cost was substantially reduced.

The Agent Incentive study (Taiwan) directly compared the systems of salary alone or salary plus bonus. In ten randomly selected counties agents received their regular salary plus a bonus, the amount of which was determined by the type of contraceptive accepted. In the control counties workers received only their usual salaries. The results showed a 14 percent level of acceptance in the experimental area as opposed to 7 percent in the control area.

In spite of this success, the question of whether to pay field-workers on the basis of the number of acceptors recruited needs further consideration in the context of specific programs. Acceptance is a definite commitment to practice contraception only in the case of sterilization. The commitment is less definite with IUDs and injectables, and very tenuous with other methods. For many clients, acceptance is never translated into practice. Nor should all acceptors be classified alike. Some are truly new acceptors who have never before used any contraceptives, while others are repeat acceptors who had previously practiced, terminated, and are now beginning again. Rather than trying to set up elaborate criteria for acceptors, it would in principle be more desirable to reward the worker on the basis of nonpregnancy, the ultimate objective of the program. A worker would receive a bonus only if the client continued to practice effectively for a certain period of time and avoided having a child for, say, two years. The question of how to implement such a scheme could be addressed in future experiments.[3] What would be the best interval for examining a woman to check for a pregnancy? Can a feasible

3. A nonpregnancy scheme proposed for Sialkot, Pakistan, was abandoned because it proved too unwieldy to implement.

way of organizing such examinations be found? Would such a scheme function better if both the workers and clients received payments for nonpregnancy? How would alternative schemes compare in cost?

Mass Media

As family planning activities became more sophisticated, greater attention was paid to the potential use of the mass media to promote contraception by providing both information and motivation. The major issue that surfaced was the sufficiency of the approach. Could the media be used alone or would they have to be supplemented by direct personal contacts? Although the experimental results have not resolved this question, they have provided some useful findings. Mass media experiments have invariably increased awareness and knowledge of family planning and, to a lesser extent, also contraceptive practice.

Some of these experiments employed only mass media, others coupled this approach with some kind of personal intervention such as home visits or group meetings. Of the experiments which used the dual approach, Sungdong Gu (Korea) offers the most conclusive results. In areas where home visits or group meetings were used in addition to mass media, acceptance rates far outdistanced those where only mass media was employed. During the first year of the experiment the acceptance rate for areas exposed only to mass media was 11 percent; for mass media plus group meetings, 15 percent; and for mass media plus home visits, 18 percent. The Kaoshiung experiment (Taiwan) relied exclusively on the mass media, however, and significantly changed attitudes and increased the knowledge and practice of family planning. The success of this undertaking paved the way for the adoption of an islandwide mass media campaign in 1972.

A fairly consistent pattern emerges in all these experiments: The level of awareness and to some extent the practice of family planning are increased; experiments which combine mass media and personal intervention are more likely to produce higher rates of acceptance; in all instances friends, neighbors, or relatives are more frequently cited as sources of information than either the media alone or the media reinforced by a home visit or a group meeting. What are the implications of this pattern? Does the fact that a peer group continues to be a major source of information attenuate arguments in favor of the mass media approach? Probably not, but the proponents of this approach are forced to examine carefully the precise way in which media operate, to investigate ways in which they can be combined with traditional communication networks, and to evaluate the cost effectiveness of the approach.

Understanding the mechanism through which mass media operate is more complex. In general, the media will reach a certain market directly, which may or may not prove to be one that was impervious to other approaches. This market must be clearly identified since its composition will largely determine the kind of media to be used. Beyond this group there is what might be termed a secondary market—those who respond not to the publicity itself but rather to a personal communication from someone who had been persuaded by the media. It is highly probable that mass media campaigns enhance and crystallize the message that is transmitted through the natural communication networks and that the media heighten the "visibility" of the subject and intensify the exchange of ideas. This is especially critical for a sensitive topic like family planning. Because the mass media are an important vehicle for the reshaping of norms, their use for the dissemination of family planning information lends legitimacy to the practice of contraception. Future experiments should seek to clarify the nature of the linkage between the media message and the traditional personal communication in the context of family planning.

The Integrated Health Approach

In the effort to advance the practice of family planning, one of the most obvious ideas was to integrate it with the prevailing system of health care, and a number of rather complex experiments were mounted to test this combination. The feasibility of this alternative was of course largely contingent on the nature of the existing health infrastructure. Linking family planning to other health care underscored the relation between the two and at the same time facilitated the delivery of services. More specific applications of the integrated health approach focused on combining family planning with maternal and child health or with usual postpartum care.

Three experiments in different parts of the world made family planning a major part of the health package in an attempt to test the impact of improved child mortality on the acceptance of family planning: the Gandhigram experiment (India), which offered sterilization, condoms, and IUDs; Danfa (Ghana), which used primarily the pill and IUDs; and Etimesgut (Turkey), which emphasized modern contraceptive methods. The results of the Gandhigram and Etimesgut experiments were encouraging. In each, the fertility indexes declined after the initiation of the project. By 1971 (after nine years) a third of the eligible couples in Gandhigram were practicing family planning; of these, two-thirds had undergone sterilization. The crude birth rate was down from 44 births per thousand population in 1959 to 32 in 1967. In Etimesgut there were significant improvements; health responded very quickly to the experimental inputs, but fertility responded less readily. A learning process was needed before family planning methods were widely accepted, and consequently improvements in fertility lagged behind those in health. In the Danfa project a 1972 survey of knowledge, attitudes, and practice showed that although

84 percent of the population knew of family planning methods, few practiced any. By 1973, one year after the addition of a family planning component, an estimated 10 percent of the eligible women had accepted.

The American Public Health Association is currently exploring new systems for the delivery of health, family planning, and nutrition services in the developing countries. This project known as DEIDS (Development and Evaluation of Integrated Delivery Systems) has recently started in Thailand; current plans call for projects in Pakistan, Ecuador, and an African country.

Other integrated experiments have concentrated on the link between maternal and child health and family planning. One of the most interesting and long run of these is the Narangwal project in India. It was designed to investigate the effect of a decline in child mortality on fertility and to test the impact of combining family planning with different packages of health services. Four combinations were tested: family planning alone; family planning plus women's services; family planning and child care; and family planning, women's services, and child services. The experiment was in operation for nine years; much valuable data was generated and now awaits analysis. The untimely termination of this experiment prevented the testing of the basic hypothesis, namely, that the experience or expectation of infant and child mortality may hinder significant movement toward lower fertility.

The postpartum approach is another attempt to introduce the notion of family planning while a woman is receiving medical attention for something else, in this case the delivery of a child. The underlying rationale is that a woman is most likely to be persuaded of the family planning message in the period immediately following the birth of a child. The International Postpartum Family Planning Program, launched by the Population Council in 1966, sought to provide information and services to postpartum patients either during their stay in the hospital or on their first postnatal visit. The focus was primarily urban women of low socioeconomic status. At its peak over one hundred hospitals representing a wide variety of cultures participated in the program, which was successful in attracting acceptors both directly and indirectly. The approach is a costly one, however, with several limitations. It is better suited to an urban setting where deliveries are more likely to be institutionalized, although in a rural setting the traditional birth attendant could certainly convey the family planning message and services. As greater emphasis was placed on the outreach approach, the importance of postpartum programs receded. An interesting variation of this concept has evolved in which family planning information and services are extended to postabortion patients. Experiments in Santiago, Chile, and in four cities in Mexico have shown that acceptance of family planning increased when patients received information and services during their hospital stay following abortion complications.

The Population Council has recently initiated experimental programs in Indonesia, the Philippines, Turkey, and Nigeria that integrate family planning with maternal and child health care. The host countries and the contracting agencies have drawn up detailed protocols governing the conduct of these projects and outlining how the data from them will be processed. Given the scope and the five-year duration of these experiments, they should furnish a wealth of data and yield some significant insights into the benefits derived from this approach. Numerous other experiments including maternal and child health, albeit on a smaller scale, have been undertaken. All indicate a significant increase in the acceptance of family planning when it is made readily available to women in the context of other health services for them or their children.

Extension techniques are another example of integrating family planning into a more general package. Multipurpose workers provide information and motivation and in some instances dispense services. The Mehrauli experiment in

India (1963–69) tested this concept.[4] Of 6,605 eligible couples, 15 percent accepted IUDs and 5 percent underwent sterilization. Given that level of practice, there was little decline in fertility; over the period, the general marital fertility rate declined from 312 to 299.

Before the integrated health approach is used in a particular area, some judgments must be made about the adequacy of the health care facilities and the extent to which they are used. An attempt should also be made to discern the prevailing attitude toward modern medicine. In traditional cultures which suspect and resist modern medical treatment it would be foolhardy to emphasize the link between family planning and health care.

Intensive Efforts and Camps

One of the earliest experimental thrusts in family planning activities was to mount all-out efforts to encourage the adoption of contraception. Large amounts of inputs were concentrated on these efforts, and the approaches tested were as comprehensive as possible. In some instances the efforts were made in addition to the regular program; in others, they took place in the absence of a program. The record shows that such undertakings have had mixed results. The Khanna project (India) provided for intensive inputs of family planning education and services through the use of field-workers who made monthly home visits. It offered premodern methods of contraception, mostly foam tablets. These merely replaced traditional folk practices and thus there was little impact on fertility or on the level of contraceptive practice. The Sweden-Ceylon (Sri Lanka) experiment and the intensive effort in Lulliani (Pakistan) yielded equally disappointing findings. Data collection in

4. This experiment was classified as an integrated approach, but it could also have been considered under "Personnel."

the Sri Lanka experiment was poorly executed; there was a very low level of contraceptive use and little evidence that fertility levels were in any way affected by the project. The intensive efforts in Lulliani included an educational campaign, home visits, and distribution of contraceptives but had a minimal impact on fertility rates. Only 7 percent of the target population accepted IUDs and the continuation rates were very poor.

The intensive campaigns in Korea, Thailand, and Iran have been quite successful. In the Korean effort the general fertility rate dropped 38 percent in the experimental area (Koyang) as opposed to 13 percent in the control area (Kimpo); when controls were used for age and parity, user rates increased from 8 to 38 percent in Koyang compared with 12 to 17 percent in Kimpo.[5]

The success of the Potharam effort in Thailand was enough to convince the leadership of the country that popular interest and acceptance of family planning was sufficient to justify the initiation of a national program. In two years the project attracted 28 percent of the eligible couples, many of whom adopted sterilization. Among those accepting IUDs there were high continuation rates, 40 percent after four years. The Intensive Multiple Service project in Isfahan met with reasonable success in rural areas, where practice of family planning increased from 5 to 11 percent, but the effort had little effect in urban centers.

The vasectomy camps in India can be viewed as a particular application of the intensive concept. Hardly experimental in the classical sense, the camps were designed to last only a short time and can be more correctly considered demonstration projects. The all-encompassing effort included publicity campaigns, educational programs, and the provision of transportation; bonuses were paid to motivators

5. Because Kimpo was included in the regular government program during the course of the experiment, the differences observed are between the experimental intervention and the regular program.

as well as to acceptors. The camps in Gujarat and Ernakulam were extremely successful. During the eight-week camp in Gujarat, ten times as many vasectomies (221,933) were done as in the preceding seven months in the state. The campaign attracted about 5 percent of the couples of reproductive age. In Ernakulam II and III a wide variety of contraceptive services was offered. As a result of the camp effort and other endeavors, the proportion of couples in the area using some method increased to about 33 percent.

The spectacular results produced by the camps in a very short period are striking, but they must be carefully evaluated. The mean age of the wife of the vasectomy acceptor was more than 28 years; the mean parity was more than 3.5 children. The lack of experience of some of the doctors performing the vasectomies, the lack of cleanliness in the camps, and the lack of medical follow-up for complications were fairly common complaints. Some people were disturbed by the ethical implications of an intensive program for sterilization, combined with high commodity or cash incentives, which in some states exceeded a month's income for many acceptors. Questions also arose as to the use of incentives as "bribes" to persuade those who otherwise might resist, and it was asked whether all acceptors were fully aware of what they were accepting. The vasectomy camps have been tried mainly in India; whether this concept is exportable remains to be seen.

Incentive Payments to Acceptors

Incentives to acceptors may be one-time payments designed to overcome barriers to acceptance.[6] Such payments

6. See Timothy King and others, *Population Policies and Economic Development* (Baltimore: Johns Hopkins University Press, 1974), pp. 99–110, for a more extensive discussion of the merits of alternative approaches to incentives.

were important in the vasectomy camps and probably account for much of their success, although it is not possible to isolate the impact of incentives from the other strenuous efforts to recruit acceptors.[7] The Ghanaian Commodity experiment also suggests that payments can be effective in increasing the proportion of women who, having been referred to a clinic, actually went there. Except in the case of sterilization, however, acceptance of a method prompted mainly by the desire to obtain an immediate incentive is likely to lead to low continuation rates.

In consequence, a small number of schemes involving deferred incentives have been started. These are generally of too recent a nature to have had any measurable demographic impact. Deferred incentive projects in India have taken the form of savings programs. In Tamil Nadu the United Planters Association of South India (UPASI) pays Rs5 into a savings account each month as long as the enrollee does not become pregnant.[8] At the age of forty-five a woman receives the deposits plus the accrued interest if she has had no more than two children. If she has had a third or fourth child she loses part of the savings; if she has a fifth child she receives no payment. Women of relatively high parity (four children) are still eligible. Approximately 90 percent of the eligible women enrolled.

There are two incentive experiments in Taiwan: The Educational Savings Program provides for annual bank deposits redeemable for certificates for postprimary education to parents with three children or less, and the Taichung Spacing Program offers free delivery for the second child plus other services depending on the length of the birth interval. (All subjects in the latter experiment are one-parity

7. For several years the regular program in India has made small cash payments to acceptors, especially of sterilization, officially described as compensation for time lost from work.

8. The Tea Estates experiment in Assam and West Bengal also offered incentives in the form of savings but of a more immediate nature than those offered by UPASI. In 1972 Rs5 was worth about US$.60.

couples, with the wife aged 15 to 29 years, who had a first child between April 1974 and March 1975.) Both of these undertakings have been well received. Two-thirds of the eligible couples initially enrolled in the Educational Savings Program; the Taichung program enrolled 75 percent of those contacted during the first eight months of operation.

These experiments have been too short-lived to indicate what their impact on fertility will be. On paper, they appear to be realistic and manageable schemes, but the setting seems to be a determining factor in their success. The social structure of the tea estates—in essence a closed community providing substantial benefits to the workers and their families—may be conducive to the implementation of the incentive scheme. A hypothesis for future research is that the success of such schemes is limited by the nature of the area where they operate. A well-defined socioeconomic entity such as the tea estates or a compact geographical area such as an island may readily lend itself to this approach, but application on a wider scale would probably produce many operational difficulties.

Other factors need to be taken into account in offering incentives for family planning. Monitoring reproductive history in a society with no registration system for vital statistics or an effective health network may prove impossible. Accurate demographic records may be difficult to obtain in places with large migratory movements. The attractiveness of an approach based on deferred monetary incentives may be attenuated by inflation unless some sort of indexing is used. And then there is the problem of motivation, with which none of the experiments has grappled. Although initially the schemes were well received, the question is whether the initial motivation can be sustained and whether a deferred incentive scheme can reinforce a desired behavioral pattern. The results of ongoing tests and further research and experimentation will, it is hoped, shed some light on these issues.

Inundation

The availability of supplies and services has been a perennial issue since the inception of family planning activities. Even after twenty years of programs and experiments, it remains a crucial consideration. The trend in the development of family planning services has been to move them out of the stationary clinical setting and bring them to where the demand exists. At present family planning services are in what might be termed the "inundation era." The prime objective of the inundation approach is to make contraceptive supplies more readily available to potential consumers.[9] Community-based distribution (CBD), village and household availability, contraceptive inundation, commercial distribution, subsidized sales, and social marketing have become the key words of this approach.[10] This community-oriented approach has been well received and has already produced its own folk heroes. As a result of his efforts to increase the use of the condom in Sri Lanka, Bandula Dadampigama has been dubbed "Uncle Preethi"—Preethi being the name under which the condom is marketed. In Thailand, Mechai Varanvaidya travels throughout the country urging the adoption of family planning and supporting efforts to make contraceptive supplies readily available. Mechai is known for his use of theatrical devices to promote the easy discussion of family planning. A favorite popularizing technique is a local balloon-blowing contest, with condoms used as balloons.

The gradual liberalization of prescription requirements

9. Some inundation experiments are reviewed separately; others are considered collectively as international community-based distribution schemes.

10. See George Washington University Medical Center, *Contraceptive Distribution—Taking Supplies to Villages and Households*, Population Reports, series J, no. 5 (Washington, D.C., July 1975).

for orals helped prepare the way for the massive distribution of contraceptives. The International Planned Parenthood Federation (IPPF) and the U.S. Agency for International Development (USAID) have played a major role in promoting this innovative approach. As of early 1977, IPPF had initiated CBD experiments in seven countries; USAID had centrally funded and monitored eleven projects of this type, and country USAID missions had initiated a number of others.

In a community-based delivery system contraceptives are sold at subsidized prices or distributed free of charge through field-workers. This approach has many variations as to what contraceptives are offered (usually orals and condoms) and how the client is resupplied. A number of CBD experiments focus on household distribution systems (such as Euiryong and Cheju in Korea) while others have made use of the mass marketing approach (Kenya/Kinga).

As can be seen from Appendix B, experiments testing the commercial distribution of contraceptives date back to the early 1960s. In some instances contraceptives have simply been added to the merchandise carried by existing commercial outlets, but even then the prices are often subsidized. In recent years commercial distribution has been widely promoted. The highly publicized Panther campaign in Jamaica has been extremely successful in increasing the sale of condoms. The record shows that when supplies are made more available, sales increase. Volume of sales is hardly a reliable indicator of proper and effective use, however, and some caution must be exercised in translating sales figures into demographic impact. In general, the distribution of contraceptives through commercial outlets makes it more difficult to collect demographic data and information on continuation rates, while household distribution schemes should facilitate the collection of such data. Since the experiments to date have underscored the success of this basic approach, future endeavors might profitably investigate ways to improve its effectiveness and to evaluate its results.

Conclusion

In an attempt to improve delivery systems, a variety of approaches have been used, all of which have some merit; but no one approach has proved itself markedly superior for general applicability. It should be noted, however, that experimentation has not been directed toward the achievement of an ideal approach but has explored such areas as the logical linkage of family planning with other health services or the effect of concentrated inputs of various approaches.

The thirty-two experiments that tested the use of a particular type of personnel in the family planning delivery system have provided the basis for some specific recommendations. The most conclusive finding to emerge was that recruitment of acceptors was most successful when workers were offered some incentive or bonus for each person recruited. To date there is no conclusive evidence as to the type of worker which would be most effective in reaching a target population. Different types of workers have been found effective in different experiments, but no experiment has compared different types of workers under different circumstances. The use of local people or satisfied users as agents of change has, however, been remarkably successful.

Experiments testing the effectiveness of mass media will probably become more numerous. In the past, mass media have been found to be most successful when supplemented with some kind of personal communication. Because mass media exercise a unique function in the molding of norms, they can be used as a legitimating device, particularly in cultures where family planning might still be viewed with suspicion. The use of mass media to heighten awareness and to generate increased demand for family planning might be combined in future experiments with home visits and community-based distribution of contraceptives. Such experiments might yield interesting results regarding both the demand for and supply of contraceptives and other family planning services.

If the purpose of experimentation is to improve the regular program, then the experimental program should be similar in nature to the regular program or should anticipate its future form. It is apparent that family planning programs are becoming more complex and multifaceted. Experiments will therefore have to address a number of approaches if they are to be germane. The question then is whether there should be one experiment combining a variety of approaches simultaneously or several experiments each testing a different type of approach. The latter alternative appears preferable because the more complex an experiment, the more difficult it is to design, manage, and evaluate.

CHAPTER 5

The Record of the Past and Criteria for the Future

THE TWO PRECEDING CHAPTERS revealed that in both the methodology used and the approaches tested past experiments have been less than satisfactory. Most did not fulfill the requirements of classical experimental design, and therefore their conclusions cannot be viewed as definitive answers to the questions investigated. Nevertheless, experimentation has had a significant impact on the development of family planning delivery systems. Experiments have answered some basic questions and have been useful in resolving field problems. They have given visibility and validity to certain approaches and thus paved the way for changes in regular programs. Though far from perfect, experimentation has been a vehicle for improving the delivery of family planning services. The issue that emerges at this juncture is: Should experimentation be continued and, if so, what priorities should be established? It is our conclusion that the usefulness of experimentation has certainly not been exhausted and could be increased by a well-defined strategy that is, to a considerable extent, the product of cumulative experience. Therefore, we have felt it worthwhile to discuss some of the merits and problems of past efforts before delineating a framework for future experimentation.

Benefits from Past Experimentation

Much of the knowledge about family planning delivery systems that is accepted without question today was accumulated over the last twenty years through experimental efforts. Initial experiments tested the acceptance of family planning as such and the effectiveness of each of the approaches considered. Although the results often needed some qualification, certain observations could be made about the effectiveness of an approach and its acceptability to the target population. These conclusions were particularly valuable since data on these subjects did not previously exist.

In addition to providing solutions, the experiments also generated new questions that became the topic of subsequent experiments. Family planning programs were initially clinic-based, but early experiments in India demonstrated that the outreach approach was feasible and established that women field-workers offering female contraceptives were effective in motivating women clients. This finding was elaborated in the Koyang/Kimpo (Korea) experiment which proved that women field-workers could also be effective promoting male contraceptives. Once the advantages of the outreach system had been recognized, the optimum type of worker remained to be determined. Experiments such as Madras Community Leaders (India), Seoul Agents (Korea), and Change Agents (Venezuela) attempted to clarify this question. Experimentation proved an ideal vehicle for testing the correlation between workers' performance and the method of payment. The evidence from the Agent Incentive (Taiwan), Worker Evaluation (Thailand), and Worker Incentive (Philippines) experiments indicated that incentive schemes usually result in higher worker output.

Experiments have made substantial contributions to the

operational aspects of national family planning programs. They have permitted program managers to explore the dynamics of delivery systems and have offered a safe medium in which to test innovations. If an approach proved successful, it could be wholly or partially incorporated into the regular program of that and other countries; if not, the negative consequences were negligible.

The record of experimentation in family planning is replete with examples of approaches that were first tried out in the experimental context and later adopted as policy. The Chulalongkorn experiment (Thailand) indicated the feasibility of using previous acceptors as motivators. As a consequence the national program adopted the idea. The Shopkeeper program in Bangladesh demonstrated the effectiveness of using commerical outlets in the community to sell contraceptives. This approach is now an accepted part of the programs in Pakistan and Bangladesh and provided the basis for more recent marketing and community-based distribution programs in other countries. The Kaoshiung mass media study (Taiwan) was the model for the islandwide mass communications campaign that began in 1972. The use of paramedicals to insert IUDs in Korea and the Mail-order Pills experiment in Taiwan were similarly adopted by the regular programs. In 1969 the Auxiliary Midwife experiment (Thailand) demonstrated that orals could be prescribed by midwives without increasing the incidence of side effects. The following year the Thai government passed a law permitting auxiliary midwives to distribute oral contraceptives.

Methodology, perhaps the most vulnerable aspect of experiments in family planning delivery systems, has also improved with the evolution of experimentation. The proportion of experiments with control groups or alternative interventions has increased during each five-year period since 1960. Although this does not guarantee that methodological standards have actually improved, it suggests that more care is being taken in the design of experiments. In some instances the conclusions of an experiment referred to the problems encountered and provided recommendations on methodology for subsequent efforts. One of the earliest experiments, the Khanna study (India), for example, pointed out that acceptance of a contraceptive did not necessarily imply its use and that acceptance could simply mean substitution of a new method for a more traditional one. The report therefore recommended that controls for these factors should be considered. Similarly, the conclusions of Koyang IUD (Korea) underscored the need for testing a hypothesis on a larger sample before accepting the results, while the results of the Santo Domingo study (Dominican Republic) demonstrated the need for using control groups.

In view of this, the question remains why more attention has not been paid to these lessons. Perhaps it is because methodology has been a secondary consideration. In some instances the objective of a demonstration or pilot project was simply to convince program authorities of the merits of the approach. Such endeavors therefore did not need elaborate statistical tests. Cost might also have been a deterrent to implementing the methodological lessons of earlier experiments. Although a more sophisticated methodology might have enhanced the validity of the results, the additional expense might not have been justified if the broad objective of an experiment could be achieved with less sophistication. Conditions in the field impose constraints that may also explain why many of the methodological flaws persist. In a sector like family planning, the perfectly designed, rigorously implemented experiment is simply not possible.

The past record reveals that, in spite of their limitations, experiments have contributed substantially to the improvement of family planning delivery systems. Furthermore, the needs of two audiences are served. If properly supervised, experimentation affords program managers the opportunity to assess the cost-effectiveness of various approaches to delivery systems. It also allows researchers to observe the differing impacts of the same interventions on contraceptive behavior and ultimately on fertility. The inherent utility of experimentation and the methodological improvements evident in the more recent efforts are thus sufficient to recommend its continued use. The sharpening of behavioral hypotheses as to the determinants of fertility can make experimentation an even more valuable tool for identifying strategies to improve family planning services than it has been in the past.

Criteria for Future Experimentation

If experimentation is to be used more effectively and the cost justified, priorities for future efforts must be carefully established and steps taken to ensure that the results can be generalized. The following guidelines are suggested.[1]

CRITERIA FOR CONTENT

Experimentation, albeit an ideal heuristic device, is not the only source of knowledge; experience and observation can also provide valuable insights and are sometimes more suitable techniques. Before an experiment is undertaken, it should be ascertained that the topic proposed for investigation is amenable to the experimental approach. Clearly, such issues as land reform and institutional reform do not lend themselves readily to the experimental process. Their impact can be observed, however, by monitoring ongoing programs. Before initiating an experiment, it should also be determined whether any large disturbing factors in the experimental environment can be isolated and whether the project is realistic in terms of cost and time.

1. Much of the material for this section comes from the discussion that took place at the Workshop on Experimentation in Family Planning held at the World Bank in May 1976.

In selecting topics for investigation some priorities must be set. Preference should be given to those items which can surmount cultural differences and those in which the potential benefits are significant. Interventions which provide services in addition to offering experimental interest should be given some priority. Attention must be paid to the methodology required for the subject selected; in essence, both substance and method must be feasible within the constraints of the experimental framework. Since it is costly to experiment on just one variable, a multivariate approach is preferable. Three major categories are suggested as fruitful possibilities for future research: approaches already known, those that have some established promise, and those that explore the nexus between socioeconomic development and fertility.

In the category of known approaches are those that have already been shown to work but that need to be refined or clarified. The following topics could be explored in greater depth: a broader definition of the role of low-level personnel in family planning delivery systems; the use of mass media on a sustained basis and the various thresholds at which behavior is affected by different combinations of media; and the impact on the efficiency of the delivery system of the distance a client must travel to receive services.

Under the heading of approaches with some established promise, one topic to be explored is lactation. This is an important consideration for both health and fertility, and there would be a substantial payoff if ways could be found to encourage newly delivered mothers to extend the lactation period. Ways of reinvigorating old methods of contraception and ways to increase the availability of abortion as a backup for contraceptive failures should also be investigated.

Various incentive and disincentive schemes have been introduced, and intermediate indicators reveal that they have substantial merit; however, considerable work remains to be done. One of the most challenging tasks would be to find existing organizational structures through which incentive schemes could be implemented.

By now it is widely recognized that emphasizing the supply of services and contraceptives is not sufficient. If fertility is to be reduced, greater attention has to be given to programs designed to change norms and modify behavior and thus alter the perceived need for additional children. The People's Republic of China has had experience with campaigns to change prevailing norms; the individual's decision to bear children has been socialized, and fertility is viewed as having ramifications for the entire community. On a more limited basis, the "Stop at Two" campaign in Korea is an example of a program designed to weaken the preference for sons and at the same time to underscore the importance of the quality of children.

It is generally acknowledged that socioeconomic development is associated with a reduction in fertility, but the linkages are far from clear. The integration of family planning services with the delivery of other social and economic services should be explored in future experiments. An effort should be made to determine better mixes of services to take advantage of the synergistic effects of combining them.

Here experiments move from the area of pure family planning services into more complex social interventions. Efforts are needed to assess the impact on fertility of such schemes as social security systems or insurance for children. Historically, declining infant mortality, better education, and increased employment of women in the modern sector have served to depress fertility. There is, however, a considerable time lag between the onset of these conditions and the observation of their impact on fertility. In attempting to discern the linkage between socioeconomic development and fertility reduction, the researcher would be well advised to study actual situations and to investigate, for example, whether fertility has fallen faster in areas served by intensive development efforts than elsewhere in the same country. Attention should be focused on isolating the factors responsible for the fall in birth rate and on trying to quantify, as far as possible, the contribution of each factor to the decline in fertility. The insights derived from such analysis would be valuable in formulating both new programs and future experimentation.

CRITERIA FOR METHODOLOGY

If the full benefits of experimentation are to be reaped, more attention must be paid to the issues of design and measurement. Just as the content of experiments must have a certain degree of universality, the methodology must also be adaptable to a variety of environments. There must be a clear statement of objectives and a precise specification of hypotheses to be tested. Ideally the design should conform as much as possible to the conditions necessary for a true experiment; this recommendation would of course have to be modified according to the purposes for which the experiment is being undertaken. If it is to be a demonstration or pilot project, a quasi-experimental design might well suffice. The measuring instruments and procedures should be as unobtrusive as possible, and every effort should be made to see that such instruments are well suited to the intervention they are attempting to measure. At the risk of stating the obvious, the experimental design should also be realistic in terms of the resources available.

The need to disseminate the results is another important consideration. From the initial stages there should be plans for writing periodic status reports. The results of the experiment should be published as soon as possible; if it is a long-term experiment, interim reports of discernible trends should be circulated. This is particularly important because it is often necessary to carry out the same experiments in various countries at different stages of development. Information on a particular type of experiment is obviously extremely useful in setting up similar undertakings. The publication of results and problems enables subsequent researchers to take advantage of the accumulated wisdom. Building on this knowledge, they will be able to design their experiments in a way that will avoid past mistakes.

In a more specific vein, the following issues should be clarified if future experiments hope to avoid the pitfalls of past endeavors.

True experiments and demonstrations. A true experiment in the family planning sector is extremely difficult to design because of the requirements for control groups and randomization. The economic, administrative, and cognitive obstacles represent formidable challenges, and the vagaries of field implementation often jeopardize the best-designed projects. It is perhaps more realistic to aim for well-designed quasi experiments. These should enable the researcher to make reasonable inferences about causality between variables and to determine if the hypothesis should be accepted or rejected. Quasi experiments are, however, less than satisfactory for determining the interactive relations among the variables, but even in true experiments this interaction often cannot be stated conclusively.

If indeed the family planning sector is more amenable to quasi experiments, the question remains as to the hierarchy of design requirements. Do all situations require a design which calls for pretest and controls and very sophisticated measurement techniques, or are there instances where a less complex design will suffice?[2] Our conclusion is that the complexity of the design is closely related to the purpose of the experiment. If previous experiments have not addressed a similar hypothesis, if the intervention itself or the setting where it is being tested is unique, and if serious policy changes are to be based on the results, a well-designed and carefully executed experiment with refined measurement instruments is in order. It goes without saying that the bet-

2. According to the Campbell-Stanley typology the possibilities range from pretest, treatment, posttest, and a well-matched control group to a one-shot intervention with neither controls nor pretests.

ter the design of an experiment, the greater the confidence that can be placed in its results. If an approach is already fairly well accepted, however, and has to be carried out in a particular environment only to prove to program managers or policymakers that it is feasible under a certain set of circumstances, then a demonstration or pilot project is appropriate. The design requirements are less rigorous, and in such situations a more fluid design is an asset since it permits modification in response to environmental changes and freedom to manipulate inputs. The results of such projects are sufficient to satisfy the needs of the decisionmakers for whom they were intended.

In summary, to meet the standards of scientific methodology the true experiment would always be preferable, but the needs of a particular sector are often satisfied with less. In view of the variety of topics and purposes, experiments in the delivery of family planning services can legitimately encompass the entire range of the design spectrum. The objectives of the experiment and the nature of the intervention should determine what type of design is needed. Fitting methodological sophistication to the situation is both a prudent and cost-effective approach to experimentation.

Duration: long and short experiments. Experiments of long duration offer several advantages not found in those with a short time span. Long-run experiments provide a better opportunity to identify the effects on fertility, while in short-run experiments it is necessary to settle for intermediate measurements of the dependent variable, which are less precise indicators of the results of the intervention. In a longer period the effects of market saturation and the initial impact of a new approach can be identified and taken into account when measuring the results of the intervention. It is also possible to measure factors other than those being tested in the intervention and to arrive at a more sensitive assessment of the mechanisms through which fertility is affected. In addition, experiments of long duration usually have more visibility and are more publicized. They tend to have impact in places other than the locality of the experiment.

On the debit side, long experiments are generally more costly, and there is a greater chance that extraneous factors will affect and possibly compromise the results. The long-run experiment may elicit less collaboration from the managers of regular programs because results are usually slow in coming and may not seem of immediate operational relevance. As in the case of design, specific situational factors—the reason for its undertaking, its objectives, and the resources available—should be decisive in determining the duration of an experiment.

Hypothesis: single and multiple. An experiment with a single hypothesis usually tests a straightforward relation, that is, the effect of a specific intervention. Most of the experiments in Taiwan have been of this type. Such projects usually yield information that is of immediate operational relevance. They are for the most part inexpensive and can be conveniently accommodated within the existing institutional framework.

Other experiments, such as those in Narangwal and Danfa, tried to answer a large number of questions simultaneously and explored a nexus of relations. Sometimes the opportunity for conducting an experiment leads researchers to add more questions than had originally been planned and the experiment may become very complicated. Multiple hypotheses offer an advantage in that the monetary cost of the experiment may increase only marginally with an increase in the number of hypotheses to be tested. By complicating the job of management, requiring the collection and analysis of additional data, and introducing the confounding effects of different interventions, however, each additional hypothesis may increase the real cost of the experiment and reduce the confidence that can be placed in the experimental results.

Complex experiments offer another advantage in that with several hypotheses there is a greater probability that some operationally relevant results will be forthcoming. Because operational relevance is of primary interest to program managers, they may be more inclined to underwrite the costs of the additional data collection. Although the cost of the experiment may thus be justified, it should be remembered that the added complexity may also attenuate the clarity of the results.

CRITERIA FOR ORGANIZATIONAL QUESTIONS

While content and methodology comprise the major substantive aspects of experimentation, procedural questions must also be considered. Where should experimentation take place? Who should fund experiments? What is the role of the researchers in relation to the program managers?

The setting for experimentation. In the past, experiments have usually taken place in countries which already had family planning programs, and there is no reason to believe that this trend will change markedly in the future. As programs continue over time, problems with the delivery system become more apparent, and experiments are undertaken to remedy this dissatisfaction. Often they take place because a new policy decision is in the offing, and the experimental setting is ideal for testing new approaches prior to adopting them as part of the regular program.

The question arises whether experiments should be carried out in countries which have no family planning programs. In such a setting experiments may be the vehicle needed to convince authorities of both the acceptability of the idea and the workability of an approach. It may be difficult, however, for the researcher to receive the needed collaboration from the government, and unless the results are positive the concept of family planning as well as the approach being tested may be discredited. This question may wane in importance as more countries adopt either an official family planning program or at least assume a posture conducive to population planning.

The pattern of interaction. An experiment is usually assumed to be mounted at the request of program managers or policymakers interested in improving or initiating the delivery of family planning services. Since financial resources and research personnel are usually scarce in a developing country, there is a dependence on foreign assistance for research activities. The introduction of foreign help often complicates the experimental setting and may exacerbate the usual friction between researchers and more operationally minded program managers and policymakers. Although developing countries need outside financial assistance, they are becoming more distrustful of the motives of foreign agencies or governments involved in research. In this setting of strained professional and national interaction, even the most methodologically sound and relevant experiment could fall victim to faulty implementation. Since this network of interaction is crucial to the execution of an experiment, it is vital that relations be improved.

Considerable effort should be expended on promoting better communication and mutual confidence between the researcher and the program manager. The views of program managers regarding the intervention should be ascertained and reflected in the experiment. This procedure would attenuate the managers' complaint that research has little operational relevance. Perhaps by locating the research unit as close as possible to the operational work, the antagonism between the two could be reduced. The uneasy relationship between researchers and managers is sometimes further complicated by the resentment of local researchers when foreign researchers are involved. When experimental efforts are funded by outside agencies, all of the critical interactions are strained even further.

The resource constraints of developing countries are not going to ease in the near future, and foreign assistance will continue to be necessary. Donor groups will, however, have to deal more perceptively with recipient countries. From the initiation of the experiment, foreign donors and researchers must realize that they are in a country by invitation and must behave accordingly. They must resist the temptation to opt for the interests of research at the expense of the welfare of the country where they are working. They must make every effort to involve qualified local researchers in the experiment. Foreign researchers should be open to suggestions from local authorities and appreciate their more intimate knowledge of both the setting and the people who will be affected by the experiment.

Before the experiment is begun, agreement should be reached regarding the lines of authority and access to the data. Perhaps the most felicitous solution to the problem of control would be to phase it gradually into the hands of local people. In the early stages advice and direction from outside sources might be needed, but a mechanism should be provided to train resident personnel so that eventually they are sufficiently qualified to take over the experiment. Of course, if trained personnel are available locally at the outset, they should be put in responsible positions with as little interference as possible. The data produced by an experiment must be made available to local researchers and in no way belong exclusively to the agency financing the research. The data and subsequent report writing should be handled with prudence and a sense of responsibility that combines a concern for research standards with a sensitivity to local circumstances. The two are far from incompatible. Unfavorable results do not have to be suppressed, but it might be wiser if they were first presented to a restricted audience of program managers or policymakers, who are in a position to remedy the conditions, rather than given immediate wide-scale distribution.

The complex professional and international relations underpinning experimentation in family planning have often been ignored in the past. It is imperative that future experimental efforts recognize and respond to this situation. More harmonious working relations between managers and researchers and between donors and recipients will promote the efficiency of the experimental approach.

Part II
The Experiments

The experiments referred to in Part I are described in detail in this section. They are arranged alphabetically by the country where they took place and, in each country, alphabetically by the name of the experiment (except in the case of Isfahan in Iran, where the experiments are in chronological order). Information on the objectives, the research design, the intervention, and the results is presented. Where estimates on cost were available, they have been included. The information is for the most part from published sources, and in many instances it is not as complete as we would have liked.

Bangladesh

The Comilla Organizer Approach

Time and place: The Organizer program began in 1961 as a pilot project in six villages and was expanded to twenty-two villages in 1964. It took place in Comilla–Kotwali Thana, an area about 100 miles square.

Institution: Pakistan Academy for Rural Development in Comilla.

Objectives: The Organizer program trained women to act as principal organizers of family planning in their villages and to sell contraceptive supplies to women.

Research design: No pretest. To ascertain the impact on fertility of this scheme as well as of the Shopkeeper program, 600 interviews were conducted from January to March 1967 in twenty villages selected from a total of 247. The reliability of the responses was checked in a second round of interviews.

Intervention: An organizer from each village was first selected and then trained for four weeks. On her return, the organizer visited women to discuss family planning and sell contraceptives (condoms and foam tablets) and to keep records on those women who purchased contraceptives. Family planning information was also disseminated by union council members, primary school teachers, model farmers, cooperative managers, and film shows.

Results: Using the Bogue pregnancy history technique, the Pakistan Academy for Rural Development analyzed fertility trends in Comilla–Kotwali Thana before and after the implementation of family planning efforts. The analysis showed that the total fertility rate declined from 8.5 in 1958–59 to 7.0 in 1963–64 and 6.2 in 1966–67. Although there were no data which directly linked this decline to the specific interventions, it was felt to be attributable at least in part to the Organizer and Shopkeeper programs.

References: Population Council, "Pakistan: The Rural Pilot Family Planning Action Programme at Comilla," *Studies in Family Planning*, no. 3 (April 1964), pp. 9–12. John Stoeckel and Moqbul A. Choudhry, "East Pakistan: Fertility and Family Planning in Comilla," *Studies in Family Planning*, no. 39 (March 1969), pp. 14–16.

The Dacca Experiment

Time and place: From 1963 to 1964 in four experimental areas in Dacca. The experiment covered 661 couples married two or more years.

Institutions: University of Dacca, Ministry of Health, and Population Council.

Objectives: To compare educational efforts addressed to three different audiences (men only, women only, or both men and women); to measure the effectiveness of each channel; to note, by consistent documentation, any observations regarding the success or failure which would be of help to the whole family planning program.

Research design: Control/test. Four semimatched groups were assigned program treatments: education for males only, for females only, or for both men and women; no educational program in the control group. Geographical clusters were isolated to make sure that no contamination took place. The population was neither a cross section of the population of Dacca nor was it randomly selected. All groups were similar in socioeconomic and demographic characteristics. Data were gathered through two surveys: one before the experiment was launched and another conducted eighteen months after the first.

Intervention: Education was offered through group meetings and home visits; posters, pamphlets, flip charts, story booklets, slides, and film strips were used. Clinics in the four areas were the source of supply. Clinic staff served only members of their own sex. Contraceptives were dispensed in the control area, but there was no special publicity or educational effort. The methods offered in all four areas included condoms, foam tablets, rhythm, coitus interruptus, sterilization, Emko, jelly, and later IUDs.

TABLE 6. PERCENTAGE OF USERS OF CONTRACEPTIVES IN EACH GROUP IN THE DACCA EXPERIMENT, BANGLADESH

Period of use and survey	*Male program*	*Female program*	*Dual program*	*Control group*
In the previous year				
Initial survey	31.5	34.5	35.1	—
Second survey	35.0	46.0	56.8	—
Ever				
Initial survey	36.9	41.2	40.5	—
Second survey	41.8	52.7	70.3	50.0
Number of couples	203	165	37	114

Results: The dual program was most effective; the channel addressed to males only was the least effective in increasing users of contraceptives (see Table 6). Improvements in percentages reflect the fact that many couples would try methods for the first time and later discontinue their use. This pattern was validated by the absence of any marked decline in either birth or pregnancy rate despite a considerable increase in the number of users during the eighteen months between surveys.

Problems/remarks: There was a limited range of contraceptives available at the time of the program. If foam tablets had not been recommended there might have been fewer pregnancies. The experiment underscored the importance of interspouse communication patterns in different subgroups. These patterns were a critical factor in determining the outcome of different educational programs; for some criteria, women showed greater improvement as a result of the educational effort aimed at males than they did in either the female or dual programs. This experiment suggests that educational efforts aimed at both sexes might well be an important way of achieving the broadest range of cognitive, attitudinal, and behavioral changes in family planning.

Reference: Oscar Alers, "Summary of Experimental Projects," Population Council, internal memorandum, 1975.

Household Distribution of Contraceptives in Rural Bangladesh

Time and place: October 1975. The treatment area consisted of 150 rural villages with a total population of 125,000. A smaller control area was selected because of the existence of good demographic data as a result of the work of the Cholera Research Laboratory.

Institution: Cholera Research Laboratory.

Objective: To assess the feasibility and effectiveness of household distribution of contraceptives.

Research design: Control/test. Treatment and control areas were chosen arbitrarily. A survey of knowledge, attitudes, and practice was conducted prior to distribution; it included 1,077 women from both the distribution and control areas. Interim surveys to determine the prevalence of contraceptives were planned for every three months during the first year and every six months thereafter.

Intervention: Field assistants were utilized to provide instructions and deliver supplies to each household. Each acceptor received a six-month supply of pills. Data collection and resupply were subsequently done by *dais* (traditional midwives) who were supervised by the field assistants.

Results: The first two surveys indicate a large increase in use. The baseline survey showed the level of contraceptive practice was only 1 percent in the intervention area; follow-up surveys indicated that 15 percent were current users. Of the 23,395 eligible women in the distribution area, 81.3 percent were contacted and 68.8 percent (13,987) of those contacted accepted a supply of six cycles of pills.

Problems/remarks: The dais who carry the supplies in a red plastic bag are becoming a familiar sight. "The lady with the red bag" may gain a symbolic identity and be a helpful reminder to village women to take their pill.

References: A. R. Kahn and D. Huber, "Household Contraceptive Distribution Programme in Rural Bangladesh: A Six-Month Experience," paper presented at the Conference on Village and Household Availability of Contraceptives, Manila, June 1976.

The Shopkeeper–Commercial Distribution Experiment

Time and place: From 1964 through 1967 in the Comilla–Kotwali Thana area, as part of a multipurpose rural development pilot project.

Institution: Pakistan Academy for Rural Development in Comilla.

Objective: The program sought to involve males as distributors to facilitate the purchase of contraceptives by men. It used existing communications networks rather than the intensive teaching that had been part of the Organizer approach.

Research design: No pretest.

Intervention: In an effort to supplement the activities of the Organizer program, it was decided to use small tea shops and other outlets by the roadside or in a bazaar to sell condoms and foam. A sign identified each shop as a place of sale. Singers and other actors performed in the villages and bazaars to make audiences aware of the family planning messages.

Results: In about three months 111 shops were selling about 1,000 dozen condoms a month; after one year 250 shops were selling about 2,000 dozen a month. An analysis of fertility trends in the Comilla–Kotwali Thana area showed that the total fertility rate fell from 7.0 in 1963–64 to 6.2 in 1966–67. Although this decline cannot be directly attributed to any specific intervention, it was felt that the greater availability of contraceptives through the distribution scheme contributed to the decline.

References: Harvey M. Choldin, "Pakistan: Shopkeeper Sales and Local Entertainment," *Studies in Family Planning*, no. 13 (August 1966), pp. 8–9. John Stoeckel and Moqbul A. Choudhry, "East Pakistan: Fertility and Family Planning in Comilla," *Studies in Family Planning*, no. 39 (March 1969), pp. 14–16.

Chile

Education/Postabortion

Time and place: From July 1, 1971, to February 28, 1972. In 1967 the Barrios Luco-Trudeau Hospital in Santiago had introduced a program for postabortion insertion of IUDs for patients requesting it, but no formal education program was provided. To fill this void twenty to twenty-five volunteers were recruited and trained in contraceptive techniques and interviewing methods. The volunteers were married females, aged twenty to sixty years, with a secondary education and from middle and upper socioeconomic groups. Supervisors maintained good contact with volunteers in order to keep them motivated.

Institutions: Asociación Chilena de Protección de la Familia (APROFA) with the support of the International Planned Parenthood Federation (IPPF).

Objective: To persuade women hospitalized for abortion complications to accept contraceptives.

Research design: Control only. Control groups which did not receive the treatment were used to evaluate the effectiveness of the program in recruiting acceptors.

Intervention: Each afternoon, Monday to Friday, volunteers gave an illustrated talk and held individual interviews to allay doubts and obtain data. Social distance was no problem. Those hospitalized after 5:00 P.M. on Friday and discharged by noon Monday were set up as a control group. Both groups were offered contraceptives at discharge, referred to a family planning clinic, and sent letters if they did not appear for an appointment. IUDs and pills were offered.

Results: The results are shown in Table 7.

Problems/remarks: Women who were given educational talks had higher acceptance rates than those who were not, and it was therefore concluded that educational activities had a positive effect on acceptance by patients. Because of the ward setting, however, there was some contamination between the two groups. Another important result was that the program showed the role of trained, motivated, and supervised volunteers.

Reference: Ellen Hardy and Karen Herud, "Effectiveness of a Contraceptive Education Program for Postabortion Patients in Chile," *Studies in Family Planning*, vol. 6, no. 7 (July 1975), pp. 188–91.

TABLE 7. PERCENTAGE OF ACCEPTORS AND NONACCEPTORS OF CONTRACEPTIVES IN THE EDUCATION/POSTABORTION EXPERIMENT, CHILE

	Group	
Category	*Experimental*	*Control*
Acceptors		
On discharge	42	36
On first clinic visit	22	16
On later clinic visit	3	3
Nonacceptors		
Reason unknown	22	36
Wishing pregnancy	11	9
Number of participants	933	491

The San Gregorio Experiment

Time and place: From 1965 to 1966 in a blue-collar area in Santiago with a population of 32,000.

Institutions: Population Council, Community and Family Study Center at the University of Chicago, and the Latin American Center for Demography (CELADE).

Objective: To evaluate family planning as a means of reducing induced abortion, fertility, and maternal and child morbidity and mortality.

Research design: Pretest. Pregnancy history was used to study changes. Variations in the age-specific fertility rate, general fertility rate, and total fertility rate were observed for a sample of women for 1962–66, the period in which the probable effects of the program would be observable. The sample classified women as patients, other protected women, and nonprotected women.

Intervention: Both education and services were offered. Information focused on the risks of induced abortion and the reliability of modern contraception. IUDs and pills were used most frequently; in some cases sterilization was recommended.

Results: The program reduced fertility. Even if extraprogram effects are taken into account there was a 19.9 percent decline in the fertility of the total sample.

Reference: Anibal Faudes-Latham, German Rodriguez-Galant, and Onofre Avendano-Portius, "Effects of a Family Planning Program in Santiago," *Demography*, vol. 5, no. 1 (1968), pp. 122–37.

Colombia

Bogotá Mail/Visits

Time and place: August 1 to August 30, 1969; Bogotá.

Institution: PROFAMILIA, a private family planning association in Colombia.

Objective: To measure the comparative effectiveness of two traditional methods of communication—personal visits and written materials.

Research design: True experiment. Lower- and middle-class women aged fifteen to forty-four with at least one child were chosen to participate in the experiment. The 881 women were randomly assigned to one of three groups: pamphlets, visits, or control. A coupon was given to the women in both treatment groups to remind them where they could obtain services and to enable the researchers to identify those who came to the clinic.

Intervention: Women in the pamphlets group simply received three pamphlets about birth control with a letter and a coupon directing them to the services at the Centro Piloto family planning clinic. The materials were delivered by messenger to their homes. The women in the visits group received home visits from a family planning worker who spent approximately ten minutes discussing family planning and encouraging them to visit a clinic. They were also given pamphlets and a coupon. The control group received no information. The names and addresses of all women entering the clinic as new patients were taken for six months after the experiment in order to identify women in the control group as well as those in the treatment groups who might have forgotten their coupons.

Results: The information campaign did not significantly affect the rate of acceptance that would have been expected in the absence of the experiment. There was a low response to both communications methods. Of the 557 women who received either the pamphlet materials or the visit, only 17 women (about 3 percent) actually went to the Centro Piloto in the six months following the communication. Several definitions of eligibility were used to derive a more detailed evaluation of the impact of the intervention. Even when all of the women classified as "unlikely to come" were removed, however, the proportion of the women who actually went to the clinic was only about 7 percent. On the whole, a high proportion of the sample appeared to be well informed on birth control.

Reference: Alan B. Simmons, "Information Campaigns and the Growth of Family Planning in Colombia," in *Clinics, Contraception, and Communication*, J. Mayone Stycos, ed. (New York: Appleton-Century-Crofts, 1973).

The Pamphlets Experiment

Time and place: November 1972 to February 1973. Sixty drugstores participated, most in Bogotá, but twenty were in small rural communities nearby.

Institution: Colombian Association for the Scientific Study of Population (ACEP).

Objectives: To make the drugstore a more up-to-date source of information about orals, suppositories, and condoms and to evaluate the effect of pamphlets on sales volume as well as on the druggists' knowledge about and attitudes toward family planning.

Research design: Control/test. The design called for control drugstores which were matched with experimental ones in terms of location and general characteristics. Sales records before the experimental intervention were monitored. Druggists were interviewed at the beginning of the intervention.

Intervention: A record of daily sales of oral contraceptives, suppositories, and condoms was kept, and at the end of every four weeks an interviewer called on each drugstore to collect sales volume for the period. If the forms were correctly filled out, the druggist received 100 pesos. After the first two months half the drugstores were given pamphlets on contraceptives to pass out to each purchaser of contraceptives. Each experimental drugstore was paired with a control store that was similar and relatively closely located. Interviews were conducted at the start of the study, and when the figures for the last month were picked up at least one druggist in each store was interviewed.

The pamphlets described how the method worked, how to use it, and the relative efficiency and health risks. There were no illustrations. Pamphlets on condoms and suppositories stated that no risk to the couple's health was involved. The pamphlet on orals advised of secondary effects and stated that, from a medical point of view, "pills are less dangerous than pregnancy."

Results: Twenty-one drugstores kept complete sales records. The introduction of pamphlets appeared related to the increase in suppository sales (statistically significant at the 0.05 level). Sale of orals in experimental drugstores was not significant; the introduction of pamphlets was associated with a significant increase in the sale of condoms. Statistical tests were used to determine if the change in volume of sales was significant for experimental and control drugstores. In pamphlet drugstores seven began to sell condoms after the study began; three after pamphlets were put in. There was an attempt to discern if the increase in sales in experimental drugstores was associated with a decline in sales in nearby control drugstores (the reason for pairing). It appeared that this was so only in the case of suppositories. Of 95 druggists originally interviewed, 65 were re-interviewed at the end of the project (34 in pamphlet stores; 31 in control drugstores) to determine changes in opinion (see Table 8). Druggists in experimental stores exhibited a greater belief in the effectiveness of orals than when the study began. They felt better able to give information about contraception than before the experiment, while control druggists felt less able even at the final interview. Pamphlets were favorably

TABLE 8. CHANGES OF OPINION AMONG DRUGGISTS INTERVIEWED IN THE PAMPHLETS EXPERIMENT, COLOMBIA

Issue	*Initial interview*	*Last interview*
Definition of family planning as birth control	43	32
Contraceptives adversely affect health of mother	85 (experimental stores)	65 (experimental stores)[a]
Contraceptives adversely affect health of child	62 (experimental stores)	24 (experimental stores)[a]
Family planning can contribute to a couple's happiness	76 (experimental stores) 87 (control)	88 (experimental stores) 87 (control)

[a] For control stores, the percentage decline was smaller.

accepted by druggists and customers; 94 percent of the druggists in the experimental group wanted to continue distributing them.

Reference: Jerald Bailey and María Cristina de Zambrano, "Contraceptive Pamphlets in Colombian Drugstores," *Studies in Family Planning*, vol. 5, no. 6 (June 1974), pp. 178–82.

PRIMOPS (Research Program in Models for Delivering Health Services)

Time and place: The design phase began in 1972, and the experiment is expected to last until 1978. Services were offered in a pilot area in September 1973 and by late 1974 reached all target areas in Union de Vivienda Popular in the city of Cali. The district has a total population of 100,000 (16,666 households) and is representative of the marginal urban areas of the region.

Institutions: Universidad del Valle, Cali Health District, and School of Public Health and Tropical Medicine, Tulane University.

Objectives: To demonstrate the feasibility of a multilevel referral system which makes extensive use of nonprofessional personnel and to improve health conditions of the demonstration area by giving special attention to medical needs in the sector of maternal and child health. The following program goals have been set: to raise nutritional standards; to lower infant mortality by 50 percent in five years; to reduce the number of unwanted pregnancies, of pregnancies of high parity women, and of induced abortions and the complications from them.

Research design: Control/test. There are three target areas and four comparison areas, matched for socioeconomic and demographic characteristics. A survey of knowledge, attitudes, and practice was conducted in both the target and control areas.

Intervention: A variety of health services are provided; simple procedures are carried out at home and at the health posts; more complex cases are referred to the health center or hospital. The unique feature of the experiment is the extension of primary health care through home visits every three months—more frequently if the situation warrants it. Home visiting is done by auxiliary nurses as well as by urban health *promotoras*, young girls from the community who receive eight weeks of training and whose primary function is to gather information about the health needs of the community. The auxiliary nurse actually delivers the health and family planning services and educates the clients in health care.

Problems/remarks: The average annual cost of the services is estimated to be about US$5 per capita. Formal evaluation of PRIMOPS is scheduled for late 1978, but because of its apparent success plans are underway to replicate the system in six other Colombian cities.

References: César Corzantes, *Summary of PRIMOPS Program*, School of Public Health and Tropical Medicine Technical Paper (New Orleans: Tulane University, February 1975). Conversation with Ramiro Delgado (July 1977), Director of International Program, Tulane University School of Public Health and Tropical Medicine.

PROFAMILIA Rural

Time and place: The pilot experiment began in 1970 in selected rural areas in the state of Risaralda. The program has gradually been expanded and is ongoing. As of 1974 there were 370 rural centers in six states distributing contraceptives and about 12,400 women had registered with the program.

Institutions: PROFAMILIA, a private family planning association, with the support of the International Planned Parenthood Federation (IPPF).

Objectives: To evaluate acceptance and use, to learn characteristics of acceptors, and to determine costs and assess the impact of the four experimental aspects of the program described below.

Research design: No pretest.

Intervention: The program was part of an integrated rural development effort that also emphasized education of the community. When a woman first accepted a method a registration card was filled out, and she was given a book of coupons marked with her registration number for use in obtaining contraceptives later. Field-workers from the area were used for communication and motivation. Condoms, spermicides, and pills were distributed by volunteer leaders in each vereda (county).

Between 1972 and 1973 four additional experimental programs were begun in the states of Risaralda and Caldas. Three augmented family planning services; the fourth sought to improve the health and nutrition of the people: (a) Vasectomy (free and at home) began in August 1973. (b) The use of aides for education, motivation, and distribution began in June 1972. (c) A cooperative drugstore project subsidized orals to members and any other person, beginning in June 1973. (d) A project to teach people how to use a pressure cooker and kerosene stove reflects PROFAMILIA's belief that a rural family planning program should be integrated into overall socioeconomic development.

Results: In three years, 6,700 women used the services of the PROFAMILIA rural program, and the continuation rate was 75.2 percent after twelve months and 60.7 percent after eighteen months. The average number of living children for each acceptor in Risaralda and Caldas was 4.1. Results of the four additional experimental projects revealed: (a) Eighteen vasectomies were performed in the first three months of the project. (b) Aides reached 18 percent of the women of reproductive age, compared with 21 percent reached by field-workers in other areas. (c) Drugstores dispensed 37 cycles of orals in June, 330 cycles in July, and 350 cycles in August. (d) There were 3,229 pairs of cookers and stoves financed with low-interest loans.

Problems/remarks: This family planning program was designed to be as simple as possible and to involve the local people as volunteers in its implementation. The cost per women-years of use was estimated at US$10.84 in 1973.

References: Gonzalo Echeverry, "Development of the PROFAMILIA Rural Family Planning Program," *Studies in Family Planning*, vol. 6, no. 6 (June 1975), pp. 142–47. Jerald Bailey and Juan Correa, "Evaluation of the PROFAMILIA Rural Family Planning Program," *Studies in Family Planning*, vol. 6, no. 6 (June 1975), pp. 148–55.

PROFAMILIA Urban

Time and place: Since March 1974 the project has been ongoing in twenty-five large urban centers.

Institutions: PROFAMILIA with the support of IPPF.

Objective: To increase sales of contraceptives.

Research design: No pretest.

Intervention: Field-workers organized posts in small shops, private houses, and police stations to provide supplies and to educate and motivate potential users. Clients filled out initial registration form. Most clients were already using contraception when they began buying supplies from these posts. Condoms, suppositories, and pills were sold to nearly 23,000 women at the beginning of 1975.

Results: Most of these 23,000 clients were buying pills. Almost three out of four people who had ever used the program were still participating in January 1975.

Problems/remarks: The cost for the first four months was US$1.42 per acceptor; by the end of the first year, only US$0.12.

Reference: Jerald Bailey, "Colombia Shows the Flag," *People*, vol. 2, no. 4 (1975).

The Radio Experiment

Time and place: February to November 1969 in two clinics in Bogotá, two in Baranquilla, and one in Medellin.

Institutions: PROFAMILIA with the support of IPPF.

Objective: To analyze the effect of radio programming on clinic attendance.

Research design: Control/test. In Bogotá and Baranquilla one clinic was associated with the radio message, the other was not. It was felt necessary to use older, established clinics where a trend line for attendance had already been established. The impact of the intervention was measured by comparing the performances of the two clinics and by comparing each clinic's record during the campaign with its previous performance. In Medellin only the longitudinal comparison was possible.

Intervention: At the peak of the campaign 33 radio stations were broadcasting twenty 30-second announcements daily.

Results: During and after the campaign in Bogotá and Baranquilla the clinics that were named in the radio message experienced an increase in the number of acceptors. The number declined in the months following the campaign but remained above the figures indicated by the previous trend. The clinic in Medellin surpassed the number of acceptors that would have been expected on the basis of its previous trend.

Problems/remarks: The use of before-and-after trend lines in analyzing the impact of the radio message helped rule out that the results could have been simply the effect of extraneous influences or seasonal variations. The similarity of the results in the three cities lends support to the conclusion that the rise in acceptor rates can be attributed to the intervention.

Reference: Elizabeth T. Hilton and Arthur A. Lumsdaine, "Field Trial Designs in Gauging the Impact of Fertility Planning Programs," in *Evaluation and Experiment*, Carl A. Bennett and Arthur A. Lumsdaine, eds. (New York: Academic Press, 1975).

The SOMEFA Experiment

Time and place: May 1974 to November 1974 in selected rural and urban areas.

Institutions: International Committee for Applied Research on Population (ICARP) and Society of Medical and Pharmaceutical Associations (SOMEFA).

Objective: To test the feasibility of promoting family planning through private physicians by offering educational material for physicians and patients, consultation, and low-cost contraceptives.

Research design: No pretest. The impact of the intervention was measured in terms of the positive response from physicians. Two treatments were tried: mailings alone and mailings preceded by a visit to the physician's office.

Intervention: Initial mailings and visits to physicians elicited approximately a hundred orders for educational materials and low-cost contraceptives. A split mailing with different prices showed that demand remained high even when prices were set high enough to meet most of the projected administrative costs. An initial visit to the physician's office, while more expensive, was more effective than a mailing alone.

Results: The approach was found to be feasible; 12 percent of the physicians contacted in small towns and rural areas purchased contraceptives or educational materials. Demand from private physicians in cities was low. Private physicians often neglected to report service statistics. An unintended consequence was that SOMEFA was called upon by the government to supply large quantities of contraceptives because government supplies had become tied up in bureaucratic bottlenecks.

The SOMEFA undertaking provided the basis for expansion of the program on a nationwide basis with emphasis on rural areas and training in sterilization (minilaparotomy) for selected physicians.

Problems/remarks: An ICARP grant of $15,063 covered the costs.

Reference: ICARP Liason Office, "ICARP Progress Report, 1973–1975" (New York: Population Council, 1976; processed).

Dominican Republic

The Santo Domingo Experiment

Time and place: From August 2 to September 14, 1971, in twelve low-income neighborhoods (barrios) in the capital city, varying in size from 1,200 to 7,000 households.

Institutions: Dominican National Council for Population and Family Planning in collaboration with Cornell University's International Population Program and with grants from the International Planned Parenthood Federation and the Pathfinder Foundation.

Objectives: To increase acceptors and to decrease dropout rates.

Research design: Control only. The experiment was carried out in barrios served by two of the city's three major clinics: the Centro Sanitario which usually had about 1,500 new acceptors a year and the Model Clinic in Moscoso Puello Hospital which had about 3,000. A third clinic, Los Minas, was selected as a control, but during the course of the experiment it introduced its own publicity campaign and had to be eliminated from the design.

Intervention: Six low-income barrios were identified around each clinic. The barrios assigned to motivators contained between 1,200 and 3,500 households; those assigned to messengers on motor bikes had about 7,000 households. Those eligible were women below fifty years of age, not enrolled in a family planning clinic, and not sterilized. After being identified the eligible women were urged to take a numbered coupon and to attend their neighborhood family planning clinic. There were 4,000 coupons numbered consecutively; one portion was filled out during the home visit with demographic and socioeconomic information, and a second part was completed at the clinic. Messengers delivered letters, promotional materials, and coupons to households according to a predetermined systematic pattern. Both eligible and ineligible women were reached. As a follow-up, messengers and motivators contacted women with appointments at family planning clinics to urge them to keep their appointment.

Results: Barrios where the motivators and messengers worked showed a 25 percent increase in acceptance over the base period and a decrease of 18 percent once the experiment terminated (after the usual seasonal increase was taken into consideration). Of 2,286 women visited by motivators, more than 60 percent were ineligible (50 percent of those ineligible were over age, 19 percent were sterilized, 13 percent pregnant, 16 percent already contracepting, and the rest were single). Of 877 eligible, 50 percent accepted and agreed to come to a clinic and 24 percent actually went. Of the 1,292 letters delivered, only 3 percent of the recipients went to the clinic. If it is assumed that the ratio of eligible to ineligible women was the same among those contacted by messenger as among those contacted by motivators, there was no difference in the rates of success between the two groups.

Problems/remarks: Motivators were not more effective

and were much more expensive than messengers. The experiment questioned the effectiveness of using individual caseworkers to motivate acceptors. The cost was US$17.00 per woman who came to the clinic as a result of a motivator visit and US$4.00 per woman who came to the clinic as a result of a messenger.

Reference: J. Mayone Stycos and A. Mundigo, "Motivators versus Messengers: A Communications Experiment in the Dominican Republic," *Studies in Family Planning*, vol. 5, no. 4 (April 1974), pp. 130–33.

Egypt

Experimental Home Visits

Time and place: The experiment began in January 1977 and is scheduled to run for eighteen months in the Bahteem area in the governorate of Qualubia.

Institution: Government of Egypt.

Objective: To see if home visits can be an effective means of improving health practices and influencing the acceptance of family planning.

Research design: No pretest. The impact of home visits was to be measured by the number of new acceptors in the treatment area compared with the number of new acceptors in the rest of the governorate.

Intervention: The plan called for home visits by teams consisting of a man and a woman from the local area. The qualifications of the team members would vary; some teams would be composed of local leaders, others would use rural health staff. Over an eighteen-month period a family would receive nine visits. The messages delivered were structured to lead gradually into the subject of family planning. The family would receive a token gift; the home visitor would receive a monetary incentive. Interim assessments of the data collected were to be made during the course of the experiment.

Results: The data available at this point show some increase in initial acceptance, but it is still too early to discern any trends in acceptance patterns. Indications are that the better trained workers are more successful in accomplishing the goals of the experiment. The token gifts to the families are not perceived as incentives and are not sufficient to motivate a couple to adopt a family planning method.

References: The World Bank, Project Appraisal Report no. 210, September 1973, and limited circulation progress reports.

Ghana

The Commodity Experiment

Time and place: A five-week period in 1970 in urban areas of Accra.

Institutions: Planned Parenthood Association of Ghana with the support of International Planned Parenthood Federation.

Objective: To evaluate the effectiveness of a simple commodity incentive in increasing the proportion of referred women who came to the clinic for service. Powdered milk was chosen as a commodity which had both real and symbolic value.

Research design: Control only.

Intervention: During the first and third week field-workers distributed a numbered gift coupon to all women interested in family planning. The coupon informed the woman that if she came within ten days she would receive a free two-pound tin of powdered milk for herself and her baby. During the second and fourth week workers distributed only the regular numbered referral slip and did not mention the free milk offer. During the fifth week free milk coupons were again offered and the workers were also offered an incentive. They would receive one point for each woman referred, three points for each one who actually came to the clinic. The worker with the most points would receive six tins of milk (the equivalent of one week's wages). A registration fee of US$1.00 was charged as a way of insuring that the woman had serious intentions of practicing and was not coming merely to receive the milk.

Results: During the control weeks the proportion of referred women who accepted was 11 percent; during the incentive weeks it was over 20 percent. During the fifth week (patient and worker incentives) acceptance was three times greater than the control weeks and 1.6 times greater than with patient incentives only.

Problems/remarks: The experiment demonstrated the attractiveness of a nonmonetary commodity incentive for both patients and workers. The presence of an incentive also shortened the interval between referral and acceptance. The cost of the commodity incentive was more than offset by the increase in the number of acceptors. During the fifth week the cost was approximately US$3.47 for each acceptor.

References: Gordon W. Perkin, "Nonmonetary Commodity Incentives in Family Planning Programs: A Preliminary Trial," *Studies in Family Planning*, no. 57 (September 1970), pp. 12–15.

The Danfa Experiment

Time and place: From 1972 to 1978 in Danfa, about twenty miles outside of Accra, with a tribally and culturally diverse population of about 60,000.

Institutions: Medical School, University of Ghana; University of California (Los Angeles); and U.S. Agency for International Development (AID).

Objectives: To test the impact of various combinations of health, maternal and child health, and family planning services in a rural area.

Research design: Control/test. An extensive baseline demographic survey and study of knowledge, attitudes, and practice were carried out initially, and a final evaluation is planned for 1978.

Intervention: The region has been divided into four areas, each of which receives a different combination of services. Area I receives all of them—comprehensive health care, health education, family planning, and the standard Ministry of Health services. Area II receives all except the comprehensive health services to test the assumption that the most cost-effective way to provide family planning services is in conjunction with an intensive educational program which emphasizes sound health practices but does not necessitate augmenting existing health services. Area III receives only the family planning program and the Ministry of Health services. This is an attempt to show that the level of acceptance necessary for a decline in fertility can be achieved without special supplementary programs and thus at a comparatively modest cost. Area IV is the control area to determine the level of acceptance of family planning in the absence of special services.

Results: Only preliminary results are available. Between July 1972 and December 1974 for every hundred women of reproductive age there were 19.4 couples accepting in Area I, 20.3 in Area II, and 10.2 in Area III. The acceptance rate for couples for all project areas was 16 percent.

Problems/remarks: Danfa was subject to high rates of in

and out migration; in the three years (1972–75) between surveys 30 percent of the samples in each area were lost as a result of migration. There was no attempt to gather economic data in the 1972 survey because it was felt that people would become "suspicious" and not respond to such enquiries. Questions on economic status were asked in the 1975 survey after the experiment had gained the confidence of the people. The sample size in each area is relatively small. The results of the intervention probably show the Hawthorne effect. An effort was made to use typical Ghanaian health workers for the delivery of services rather than recruiting special people for the experiment. The experiment has brought about many innovations in the delivery of health services and family planning, especially the use of nurse midwives to insert IUDs at home. The total cost is approximately US$5.6 million. The objectives of the experiment have been modified to focus more on operationally oriented goals than on pure research.

References: Conversation with Peter Heller, consultant to AID evaluation team that visited Danfa early in 1975. Also Henry M. Gelfand, David T. Allen, Peter S. Heller, Douglas H. Huber, Godwin K. Nukunya, and Roger J. Poulin, "An Evaluation of the Danfa Comprehensive Rural Health and Family Planning Project in Ghana" (Washington, D.C.: American Public Health Association, 1975; processed), no. 146. D. A. Ampofo, D. D. Nicholas, S. Ofosu-Amaah, S. Blumenfeld, and A. K. Neumann, "The Danfa Family Planning Program in Rural Ghana," *Studies in Family Planning*, vol. 7, no. 10 (October 1976), pp. 266–74.

Greenland

The Greenland Experiment

Time and place: The program began in autumn 1967 in the Narssaq district of southern Greenland, with a population of 1,925.

Institution: Health Service of Greenland.

Objective: To promote insertion of IUDs; prior to the campaign only condoms were available.

Research design: No pretest.

Intervention: Articles in newspapers, posters in hospitals, lectures, and other publications to promote IUD insertion.

Results: By the end of the first year 113 IUDs had been inserted. Between November 1967 and July 1969 there were 158 insertions, six of which were reinsertions and only seven of which were discontinued before the end of six months. Of the 451 adult women in the test area in 1967, 33 percent had accepted IUDs two years later. The birth rate decreased from about 45 to 20 per thousand between 1967 and 1969.

Reference: Ole Berg, "IUDs and the Birth Rate in Greenland," *Studies in Family Planning*, vol. 3, no. 1 (January 1972), pp. 12–14.

Honduras

Acceptor Agents

Time and place: From July 1972 to June 1974 in Tegucigalpa, the capital of Honduras.

Institution: International Committee for Applied Research on Population (ICARP).

Objective: To increase the acceptance of oral contraceptives through a program of home visits.

Research design: Control only. The experimental barrios consisted of those that had a community agent (*paciente visitante*) assigned to them. The comparison areas were all other barrios where obstetrical and abortion cases lived. The two types of barrios were quite similar, but no relevant data were analyzed and no standardization procedures were applied.

Intervention: Previous acceptors of oral contraceptives were used as community agents to recruit postpartum and postabortion patients as pill acceptors. Motivators approached patients in hospitals; community agents visited women in their homes within one month of discharge to encourage and resupply old acceptors and to recruit new ones.

Results: Between January 1973 and June 1974, 41 percent of the patients in the experimental barrios had accepted oral contraceptives compared with 25 percent of the patients in the reference areas. Program continuation rates were higher for the experimental barrios; by international standards the rates for both areas were quite low. The experiment indicated that resupply by neighborhood agents rather than by the clinic increased the effectiveness of the program.

Problems/remarks: Since pills were given away free, there was less acceptor commitment. Higher rates of participation do not necessarily imply higher rates of contraceptive protection.

Reference: J. Oscar Alers, "Summary of Experimental Projects," Population Council, internal memorandum, 1975.

Hong Kong

Field-workers

Time and place: Four months in 1966 in the Resettlement State.

Institutions: Social Survey Research Center, Chinese University of Hong Kong, and Family Planning Association of Hong Kong with the support of IPPF.

Objective: To find the difference in effectiveness between (a) a brief home visit by a field-worker to provide information and encourage the client to visit a clinic and (b) a long visit by highly qualified staff members to consider social, personal, and economic problems of clients.

Research design: True experiment. A preliminary census located married women under fifty who were living with their spouse and were neither pregnant nor practicing family planning. This target population was divided into three groups: one received the comprehensive approach, one the traditional approach, and the other was the control. All the women who went to the clinic and a small sample of nonattending women were interviewed to discover why they did or did not attend.

Intervention: The comprehensive interviews and the brief traditional visits were made over a period of two months. In the third month the control group was divided into three subgroups that repeated the original research design, and visits were made as in the first two months. The method offered was the IUD.

Results: Of 1,432 women visited, 88 went to a clinic. The percentages of women visited who attended a clinic were:

Time	*Comprehensive*	*Traditional*	*Control*
First two months	8.5	3.8	1.0
Last month	7.3	1.9	0.0

The comprehensive approach took an average of 6 hours and 5 minutes to result in a clinic visit, while the traditional approach averaged 3 hours and 46 minutes. The comprehensive approach was more effective among women with small families. Women who wanted more children were unlikely to accept introductory slips for IUD insertions.

Reference: Robert E. Mitchell, "Hong Kong: An Evaluation of Field Workers and Decision-Making in Family Planning Programs," *Studies in Family Planning*, no. 30 (May 1968), pp. 7–12.

The Reassurance Experiment

Time and place: From April 1968 to January 1969 in clinics under the auspices of Hong Kong Family Planning Services.

Institution: Hong Kong Family Planning Services.

Objective: To determine whether home visits to offer reassurance would significantly reduce the number of IUD removals. If so, clinic policies could be revised to include techniques to reassure clients and thus improve IUD retention rates.

Research design: True experiment. IUD acceptors at all clinics were assigned alternately to either the experimental or the control group. There were 1,453 in the experimental group and 1,583 in the control group for a total of 3,036. Interviews took place during August and September 1969 to supplement clinical records. Neither the clinic staff nor the interviewer knew to which group an acceptor belonged.

Intervention: It was felt that the first fifteen days after insertion of an IUD is the period of greatest stress when removal is most likely. Welfare workers therefore made home visits to reassure IUD acceptors in the experimental group within ten days after insertion. They reminded patients to visit the clinic six weeks after insertion for a checkup and encouraged them to consult the medical staff at the clinics if they were worried.

Results: The number of removals because of side effects was reduced by reassurance home visits, as was the overall rate of removal for medical reasons. The difference between the number of removals in the two groups was significant after the third month, but by the twelfth month the difference was no longer significant. In the first year after the insertions there were 161 removals in the experimental group and 200 removals in the control group.

Problems/remarks: The project had little long-term effect on IUD users. The principal positive result was that these women were more likely to recommend IUDs to friends. The advantages obtained by the program were not sufficient to justify the heavy investment in services, and the project proved too costly to be adopted.

Reference: K. C. Chan, "Hong Kong: Report of the IUD Reassurance Project," *Studies in Family Planning*, vol. 2, no. 11 (November 1971), pp. 225–33.

India

Acceptance of Orals

Time and place: From November 1968 to June 1970 in three clinics in the Howrah district of West Bengal: one in the central city of Howrah, one in a slum area of the same city, and a rural clinic seven miles from town. Each clinic served about 10,000 people. The majority of eligible women in the rural and slum areas were illiterate.

Institutions: Humanity Association and Pathfinder Fund.

Objective: To compare the acceptability and effectiveness of oral pills among women in urban, rural, and slum areas.

Research design: No pretest.

Intervention: Contraceptives were distributed by the clinics free of charge. Field-workers made repeated home visits to eligible couples to register them, to convince them to go to the clinics, and to make clinic appointments. In urban areas the program had been publicized before initiation. In cases of rejection or broken appointments social workers made two or more attempts at persuasion. If there

TABLE 9. ACCEPTANCE OF ORAL CONTRACEPTIVES AND CONTINUATION RATES AMONG URBAN, RURAL, AND SLUM WOMEN IN WEST BENGAL, INDIA

Place	*Observations*	*Number of acceptors*	*Percentage accepting*	*Percentage of acceptors continuing* 12 cycles	18 cycles
Urban	Majority were acceptors prior to visit	609	42.7	77.6	66.7
Rural	Most accepted after one contact	318	24.4	87.7	85.1
Slum	Most accepted after two contacts	474	31.8	47.4	33.3

were no contraindications the woman was given oral contraceptives.

Results: The results are shown in Table 9.

Problems/remarks: The cumulative continuation rates were highest for rural areas; slum acceptors showed the highest drop-out rates. The experiment demonstrated that women in rural areas, who are likely to be illiterate, will accept the pill.

Reference: Murari Majumdar, B. D. Mullick, A. Moitra, and K. T. Mosley, "Use of Oral Contraceptives in Urban, Rural, and Slum Areas," *Studies in Family Planning*, vol. 3, no. 9 (September 1972), pp. 227–32.

The Andhra Pradesh Nirodh Fortnight

Time and place: From December 26, 1970, to January 10, 1971 (fifteen days), in the state of Andhra Pradesh.

Institutions: The government of India and the distribution networks of several companies: Brook Bond Tea, Hindustan Lever, India Tobacco, Lipton Tea, Tata Oil Mills, and Union Carbide.

Objective: To study the impact of personal contacts on the increased awareness and use of Nirodh condoms.

Research design: No pretest.

Intervention: During the experimental period about 6,500 field-workers visited 2.4 million couples in 28,000 villages and towns in the state. The campaign received wide coverage in the media.

Results: Free samples were accepted by 1.7 million couples. The Operations Research Group conducted a survey in mid-1971 to evaluate the impact of this intervention, but the results of this survey are not available.

Reference: Anrudh K. Jain, "Marketing Research in the Nirodh Program," *Studies in Family Planning*, vol. 4, no. 7 (July 1973), pp. 184–90.

Ernakulam I

Time and place: November and December 1970 in Ernakulam, a district of Kerala with a population of 2.38 million in 1971. The main camp—set up at Cochin, a port city of the district—operated for the entire month of the campaign. A week-long subcamp was held at Thodupuzka, a town in the outlying area. There were 300,000 eligible males (defined as those with wives of reproductive age).

Institutions: The campaign was financed by funds from the central government, Kerala state government, CARE, panchayats (village councils), and public contributions.

Objective: To obtain 15,000 sterilizations.

Research design: No pretest. Data were collected for later study.

Intervention: The district was divided into units, and a list of eligible persons in each was prepared. Each unit was assigned its own target and given a day in the camp. Publicity and education campaigns were initiated in each subdivision about two weeks before camp day, with special emphasis on the day before the trip to camp. Public meetings, small group discussions, loudspeakers, posters, and all the radio stations were used in the campaign. Operations were performed in cubicles set up in the camps. Cash and other incentives were offered to acceptors and promoters.

Results: There were 15,005 vasectomies performed, which was 1.4 times the maximum annual achievement in the district. The mean age of vasectomized men was 38.9; the wife's mean age was 32.2.

Problems/remarks: The camp atmosphere reinforced the social acceptability of sterilization and to a great extent allayed the patients' anxiety. Some doctors were not very experienced, however, and often there were long waits and unsanitary facilities. Some clients from outside the district had to walk back home, thus increasing the incidence of complications. The cost was Rs113 (US$15) per vasectomy and Rs65 (US$9) per birth averted. A statistical model adjusted for the age distribution of male acceptors of sterilization was used to estimate the number of births that would have been expected in the absence of contraception. It was estimated that each male sterilization at the first camp prevented 2.0 future births and at the second camp 2.1.

Reference: S. Krishnakumar, "Kerala's Pioneering Experiment in Massive Vasectomy Camps," *Studies in Family Planning*, vol. 3, no. 8 (August 1972), pp. 177–85.

Ernakulam II

Time and place: July 1971 in the district of Ernakulam.

Institutions: Kerala state government, the District Family Planning Bureau, and the panchayats.

Objective: To provide sterilization services (primarily vasectomy).

Research design: No pretest. Data were collected for a later study.

Intervention: Similar to Ernakulam I.

Results: There were 62,913 vasectomies and 505 tubectomies performed. The mean age of the vasectomy acceptors was 37.4 years; the mean age of their wives was 30.8.

Problems/remarks: Each vasectomy cost Rs145 (about US$20). The cost per acceptor in both Ernakulam I and II was thus higher than the cost under the regular program during the three preceding years (Rs104 or about US$14).

Reference: S. Krishnakumar, "Kerala's Pioneering Experiment in Massive Vasectomy Camps," *Studies in Family Planning*, vol. 3, no. 8 (August 1972), pp. 177–85.

Ernakulam III

Time and place: July and August 1972 in the district of Ernakulam.

Institutions: Kerala state government, District Family Planning Bureau, and panchayats.

Objective: To provide sterilization and IUDs.

Research design: No pretest.

Intervention: Although the intervention was similar to that of Ernakulam I, in this case several camps were held simultaneously in seven subdistricts, and vasectomies, tubectomies, and IUDs were offered.

Results: About 15,285 vasectomies and 291 tubectomies were performed, 1,120 IUDs were inserted, and some people accepted condoms. The mean age of an acceptor of sterilization was 35.1 years; the mean age of the wife was 28.1. After Ernakulam III 32.7 percent of the district's eligible couples were protected by some method of family planning.

Problems/remarks: Rs125 (US$17) per acceptor.

Reference: S. Krishnakumar, "Ernakulam's Third Vasectomy Campaign Using the Camp Approach," *Studies in Family Planning*, vol. 5, no. 2 (February 1974), pp. 58–61.

The Gandhigram Experiment in the Athoor Block

Time and place: Various programs to improve rural life were conducted in the Athoor Block between 1952 and 1971. (A block is an administrative grouping of panchayats, the smallest unit of self-government, for purposes of community development.) A family planning component was added in 1962 in Gandhigram in the district of Madras. According to the 1961 census, the total population was 100,606; 64 percent of the people were in agriculture, and 40 percent of the heads of households had no formal education. Eighty-six percent of the people were Hindus, 10 percent Christians, and 4 percent Muslims.

Institutions: Gandhigram Institute of Rural Health and Family Planning and the government of Tamil Nadu.

Objectives: To understand community dynamics and to make contraceptive supplies easily available through village depots.

Research design: Control/test. The program developed in stages. At each stage a group of villages was incorporated and baseline surveys were made. A system was set up to record vital statistics. Service statistics were recorded, and a panel study of selected households was carried out over time.

Invervention: A major family planning component was added to the health package. Workers were paid at about double India's usual salary rates, and worker-to-population ratios were high: one auxiliary nurse-midwife per 10,000 people, one family planning worker per 20,000, and one woman health visitor per 40,000. At the block level there was an additional woman doctor and extension educator. After 1965 there was an even higher staff-to-client ratio. Extensive training efforts were undertaken. The IUD was introduced in 1965; the tubectomy effort was extended in 1967.

Results: In 1971, 34 percent of the eligible couples (19,714) had accepted some method of contraception—16 percent vasectomy, 7 percent tubectomy, 8 percent IUDs, and 3 percent condoms. The crude birth rate was reported to have declined from 43 births per thousand in 1959 to 31.3 per thousand in 1971.

In a social experiment as comprehensive as this, it is difficult to establish a direct cause-effect relation between program activities and the decline in fertility. Studies by the Gandhigram Institute indicate that a maximum of two points in the decline of the birth rate could be attributed to the family planning intervention. Changes in the age structure or in marital patterns could also affect the birth rate, which reflects the impact of social and economic development programs in the area as well.

Reference: K. A. Pisharoti, K. V. Ranganathan, S. Sethu, and P. R. Dutt, *The Athoor Experience: Implications for a Statewide Family Planning Program* (Madurai, Tamil Nadu, and Chapel Hill, N.C.: Gandhigram Institute of Rural Health and Family Planning and Carolina Population Centre, 1972).

The Gujarat Experiment

Time and place: From November 1971 to January 1972 in Gujarat, a state with a population of 27 million.

Institutions: Government of Gujarat and the state Family Planning Bureau.

Objective: To perform 150,000 vasectomies.

Research design: No pretest. There was a good registration of acceptors for purposes of data collection and follow-up.

Intervention: About 1,000 small camps were set up around the state; the main camps in each district were permanent, and mobile minicamps eliminated the need for transportation of clients and were more cost-effective. Acceptors were visited forty-eight hours after the operation, then once a week for a month, and once a month for a year. Tubectomies were performed not at the camp sites but in local hospitals under the regular program. Acceptors of tubectomies did not receive the incentives offered to vasectomy acceptors. Both acceptors and motivators received incentives which were lower than those offered in Ernakulam, but higher than those offered as part of the regular program. Advance planning, a recently prepared register of eligible couples, the publication of a scoreboard in newspapers to encourage competition among districts, cultural programs, and mass publicity were important elements in the success of the camp.

Results: About 222,000 vasectomies were performed; the total number of sterilizations done during the campaign (232,000) was approximately 1.6 times the annual sterilization target for Gujarat.

Problems/remarks: Gujarat demonstrated that the use of multiple camps located throughout the state rather than a single massive camp at district headquarters would not only extend coverage but also facilitate the diffusion of family planning information. Most previous studies showed a higher rate of literacy among acceptors of sterilization than that found at Gujarat where about 65 percent of the acceptors were illiterate. Gujarat thus demonstrated that the illiterate and rural poor will accept sterilization.

Reference: V. H. Thakor and Vinod M. Patel, "The Gujarat State Massive Vasectomy Campaign," *Studies in Family Planning*, vol. 3, no. 8 (August 1972), pp. 186–92.

The Hooghly Experiment

Time and place: From April through June 1966 (sixty-three days) in the major urban areas of three cities in West Bengal, consisting of more than 400 blocks of about 150 households each. The people were low-income industrial workers.

Institutions: Ministry of Information and Broadcasting at the national level and its counterpart in the district of Hooghly.

Objective: To evaluate an intensive publicity program to introduce the IUD.

Research design: Pretest. Two sets of 24 blocks were selected systematically for baseline surveys before the campaign. All the married couples with wives aged fifteen to forty-four were listed and stratified, and every fourth couple in each stratum was chosen. Both husband and wife were interviewed—524 wives and 555 husbands in all, the wife three or four days before her husband. Another survey after the campaign interviewed 538 wives and 571 husbands.

Intervention: Cinema slides at movie houses, film projections, group meetings, radio broadcasts by prominent persons, outdoor posters, articles and ads in newspapers, and literature distributed at clinics were used to publicize family planning, but exhibitions were the focal point of the entire campaign. Although the emphasis was on IUDs, conventional methods were also available.

Results: The overall coverage was substantial; about three-quarters of the men were reached and almost two-thirds of the women. Street posters accounted for the greatest share of exposure. The impact of the publicity was greater on wives; the number of women with knowledge of some method of contraception increased from 51 to 69 percent of the total, whereas the number of men increased only from 48 to 60 percent. The overall percentage of those practicing some form of birth control went up, but there was little change in the percentage practicing among those who already had some knowledge before the campaign.

Problems/remarks: The Hooghly campaign demonstrated again that intensive media efforts can successfully educate their target groups. Such efforts are less successful, however, in increasing the motivation to practice among those who are already informed.

Reference: T. R. Balakrishnan and Ravi J. Matthai, "India: Evaluation of a Publicity Program on Family Planning," *Studies in Family Planning*, no. 21 (June 1967), pp. 5–8.

The Khanna Experiment

Time and place: From 1953 to 1960, with a follow-up in 1969. The sixteen villages participating had a population of 16,000 in 1960. The seven test villages had about 1,000 eligible couples.

Institutions: Harvard University, Christian Medical College of Ludhiana, government of India, United States Public Health Service, Population Council, and Indian Council of Medical Research.

Objectives: To determine if the rural couples in India could practice a single contraceptive method effectively enough to reduce significantly the growth rate of the population, and to evaluate factors affecting fertility. The targets were to increase acceptance and the effectiveness of contraceptives in order to reduce the birth rate from 40 to 35 births a year per thousand population.

Research design: Control/test. There was a baseline survey and a monthly collection of data and verification of births and deaths. In the test area and in one control area the data were collected directly from the people themselves, and in another control area, from village officers. The experiment took place in three stages: exploratory, pilot, and definitive in seven test villages; there were nine control villages.

Intervention: Doctors, social workers, and field-workers (one male and one female per 1,500 population) met with husbands and wives monthly to provide family planning education and supplies. Medical care was also given on request. During the exploratory stage several traditional contraceptives were offered, and foam tablets were selected for use in the experiment.

Results: After two and a half years 17 percent of the couples had established themselves as contraceptors and 45 percent had used contraception at one time or another. Maximum use at any time was 30 percent. The outcome fell short of the project's target and was insufficient to affect the birth rate.

Problems/remarks: The expansion of wheat cultivation and migration may have reduced the population pressure. The foam tablets were ineffective and practice was not continuous. In addition, the tablets were probably substituted for some other method that would have been used in the absence of the experiment. The annual cost for the total project was Rs197,000 (US$42,000 in 1960); the family planning component cost about Rs80,000 (US$17,000).

References: Population Council, "India: The India-Harvard-Ludhiana Population Study," *Studies in Family Planning*, vol. 19, no. 1 (July 1963), pp. 81–96. John Wyon and J. B. Gordon, *The Khanna Study* (Cambridge, Mass.: Harvard University Press, 1971).

Madras Canvasser

Time and place: From 1959 to 1968 in the state of Madras.

Institution: Government of India.

Objective: To increase the number of vasectomy acceptors by using locally recruited and vasectomized canvassers.

Research design: No pretest.

Intervention: Beginning in November 1959 payments of Rs10 (US$1.33) were made to canvassers in Madras City and to the panchayat organizations in rural areas for each man recruited, but these payments were abolished in April 1963. Originally canvassers attached to Madras city clinics were restricted to urban areas; this restriction was lifted after August 1965. Canvassers were also affiliated with district health centers and primary health centers.

Results: Madras had the highest number of sterilizations (3.42 per 1,000 population) of all Indian states during the period when the fee system was operative. Canvassers were effective, allowing a benefit-cost ratio estimated at 5:1 and probably greater.

Problems/remarks: The recruiting activities of canvassers were highly criticized. In their zeal to recruit cases, the canvassers often misrepresented the nature of the operation, brought men with less than three children, and sometimes defrauded the patient out of his share of the incentive for accepting a vasectomy.

Reference: Robert Repetto, "A Case Study of the Madras Vasectomy Program," *Studies in Family Planning*, no. 31 (May 1968), pp. 8–16.

Madras Community Leaders

Time and place: The experiment began in six villages in 1962 and expanded to 59 more in 1965, covering a population of 55,000. The villages were deliberately chosen because of the absence of undue friction or religious objection to the experiment. They were comparatively high in socioeconomic status and considered good for demonstration purposes.

Institution: Gandhigram Institute of Rural Health and Family Planning.

Objective: To demonstrate the effectiveness of village leaders in promoting family planning and distributing contraceptives.

Research design: No pretest. The changes in contraceptive practices over the period of the intervention were used to indicate the impact of the treatment.

Intervention: The leaders were selected after interviews in the community. They were trained, provided with help from regular staff members, and remotivated about twice a year. They were given as much responsibility as possible. Condoms and vasectomies were the principal contraceptive methods offered.

Result: A dramatic increase in the acceptance of family planning was observed about one year after the initiation of the program.

Reference: Population Council, "India: The Use of Community Leaders to Promote Family Planning," *Studies in Family Planning*, no. 13 (August 1966), pp. 6–8.

The Meerut Experiment

Time and place: From May 1966 to September 1966, about four months, in the Meerut district in Uttar Pradesh. The northern part of the district is rural, the south is industrial. The population in 1961 was 2.7 million; in 1966, 3.1 million. There were 26 community development groups, each one covering about 50 panchayats (village councils).

Institution: Central Family Planning Institute of New Delhi.

Objective: To see if a low-keyed family planning information effort would raise the level of knowledge about family planning programs and services.

Research design: No pretest. Surveys were conducted in May and September 1966, before and after the intervention, in eight rural villages and eleven urban areas to determine the extent of knowledge of family planning services. There were very few interviews: 115 in rural and 170 in urban areas.

Intervention: The program included simply written materials distributed by mail, special materials for areas where IUD insertions were available, cinema slides in movie houses, newspaper ads, and point-of-sale materials for retail outlets selling condoms at government-subsidized prices.

Results: There was some increase in knowledge of family planning services. Sales of condoms and the number of sales outlets also increased. In general, the low-cost campaign was successful.

Reference: B. L. Raina, Robert Blake, and Eugene M. Weiss, "India: A Study of Family Planning Communication, Meerut District," *Studies in Family Planning*, no. 21 (June 1967), pp. 1–5.

The Mehrauli Experiment

Time and place: From 1963 to 1969 in 33 villages of a rural community development block near Delhi.

Institution: National Family Planning Institute, Delhi.

Objectives: To test the application of extension techniques in rural areas, to demonstrate changes in fertility, and to provide field practice for the National Family Planning Institute in Delhi.

Research design: Pretest.

Intervention: Extension techniques were used to provide information and services; IUDs and sterilization were offered.

Results: Of the 6,605 eligible couples, 15 percent accepted IUDs and 5 percent accepted sterilization. There was little recognizable decline in fertility to accompany the level of practice reported. Between 1963 and 1969 the crude birth rate fell from 49.6 to 47.0 births per thousand population; the general marital fertility rate (that is, the total number of live births a year per thousand married women aged fifteen to forty-nine) went from 312 to 299.

Reference: Population Council, unpublished appendix to Bernard Berelson and Ronald Freedman, "The Record of Family Planning Programs," *Studies in Family Planning*, vol. 7, no. 1 (January 1976).

Multipurpose Worker

Time and place: 1970 in Uttar Pradesh.

Objective: Multipurpose workers trained in health, agriculture, and family planning were used to motivate the population and to deliver contraceptives.

Research design: No pretest.

Intervention: The area was divided into intensive districts, where villages were visited once a week, and extensive districts, where visits were made once a month or even less frequently and no individual contacts were made for family planning. Male and female teams of workers, who had already gained credibility or acceptance in the field of agriculture or health, were assigned to areas with a population of about 20,000. The teams established rapport before bringing up family planning. If a couple adopted family planning, follow-up was provided. It was intended that an intensive village would become a "maintenance" area when a government field-worker was assigned there, or when a threshold of acceptance was reached so that only delivery of contraceptives was required, or if the village was not responding. Field-workers maintained standardized monthly reports, and registers of target couples were processed at the Carolina Population Center. The contraceptive methods available included orals and condoms. Referrals were made for sterilizations or IUD insertions.

Reference: D. Oot and M. Russell, "Family Planning Delivery Systems: An International Survey" (New York: Population Council, 1975; processed).

The Narangwal Experiment

Time and place: From 1966 to 1974 in twenty-six Punjab villages with a population of 35,000. The rapid socioeconomic development of the area during this period permitted an analysis of the interactions among health, population, and other development sectors.

Institutions: World Health Organization; U.S. Agency for International Development; U.S. Department of Health, Education, and Welfare; Indian Council of Medical Research; and Johns Hopkins University.

Objectives: To measure the impact of combining family

planning with several integrated packages of health and nutrition services. Also, to test the "child survival hypothesis," which asserts that a decrease in infant mortality will ultimately bring about a decrease in fertility as parents perceive that fewer births are needed to assure the survival of a desired number of children to maturity.

Research design: Control/test.

Intervention: Different packages of services were offered to four experimental groups: (a) family planning, women's services, and child care, (b) family planning and women's services, (c) family planning and child care (this group was also part of a nutrition project and therefore received nutritional inputs), and (d) family planning services and family planning education. A control group received no services.

Results: During the first two years the rates of acceptance were remarkably similar in all treatment groups. Current user rates in group (d) were initially quite high but later leveled off. The effective user rate (the current user rate corrected for effectiveness of the contraceptive used) is probably the best indicator of the protection from pregnancy provided by the family planning program in the experimental groups. Table 10 shows the current users as a percentage of the total eligible couples for the four experimental groups at selected intervals.

The crude birth rate, total fertility rate, and general fertility rate appear to have declined in the experimental villages between 1969–70 and 1973, with a rapid decline for treatments (a), (b), and (d) and a slower one for treatment (c). The adjusted figures for the control villages show no change in fertility levels over the same period, but there is no justification for attributing the lower fertility to the experimental treatment. It is difficult to assess a fertility change that has taken place in such a short time, particularly when—as in the case of Narangwal—the rates were based on a small

TABLE 10. CURRENT USERS OF CONTRACEPTIVES AS A PERCENTAGE OF ELIGIBLE COUPLES IN THE NARANGWAL EXPERIMENT, INDIA

Experimental group	*Year family planning services began*	*Duration of service*		
		21 months	*39 months*	*54 months*
Family planning, women's services, and child care	1969	22	26	34
Family planning and women's services	1969	25	34	41
Family planning and child care	1970	27	28	—
Family planning and education	1972	30	—	—

population size, the experimental and control villages differed substantially in caste composition, and the procedures for data collection were not uniform in the experimental and control areas.

Because of strained relations between the United States and India, the experiment terminated sooner than anticipated. It therefore could not be ascertained whether perceptions of child survival had changed and, if so, whether this perceived change altered fertility.

Problems/remarks: The project report cited many difficulties: (a) Delays in completing parts of the experimental design caused problems that were exacerbated by the unexpected early termination of the project. (b) Continuing changes in the pattern of services provided made analysis difficult. (c) The collection of accurate vital statistics was hindered by the practice of village exogamy. (d) The experimental groups were too small. (e) The lack of a strong Indian institutional base was often politically embarrassing and functionally disruptive. (f) There was a failure to grasp the implications of political developments for the project's future. (g) Because this was a relatively short-term international project, the Indian staff viewed it as having little career potential, and there was an extensive turnover of personnel at all levels.

Reference: Rural Health Research Center, *The Narangwal Population Study: Integrated Health and Family Planning Services* (Narangwal, Punjab: 1975).

The Nirodh Experiment

Time and place: Ongoing since September 1968 in all of India.

Objective: To extend the scope of the family planning program.

Research design: No pretest. Two forms of marketing research were used to evaluate the impact of the scheme: analysis of monthly sales to wholesalers and retailers and consumer research among 26,000 randomly and representatively chosen couples who were interviewed for knowledge, attitude, and practice.

Intervention: Three different schemes were used to distribute Nirodh condoms: (a) a commercial scheme in which the government sold Nirodhs to major distributors who in turn sold them to retailers for resale to customers; (b) a free distribution scheme in which workers for the Public Health Service visited homes of eligible couples and offered them Nirodhs free; and (c) a "depot holder" scheme in which Nirodhs were supplied free to selected depots (mainly post offices in remote rural areas) which could then sell them at a low price. Point-of-sale advertising and a large publicity campaign characterized this program.

Results: Average monthly consumer purchases of

Nirodhs (in millions) were: January 1970, 2.6; July 1970, 3.3; April–June 1971, 4.7; October–December 1971, 5.7; January–March 1972, 6.0.

Reference: Anrudh K. Jain, "Marketing Research in the Nirodh Program," *Studies in Family Planning*, vol. 4, no. 7 (July 1973), pp. 184–90.

The Singur Experiment

Time and place: From 1954 to 1965 in the villages of West Bengal, close to Calcutta.

Institution: All-India Institute of Hygiene and Public Health.

Objective: To measure changes in knowledge, attitudes, and practice of family planning and in birth rates.

Research design: Control/test. A baseline survey was made, and vital statistics were registered in eight experimental villages (7,500 people) and fifteen control villages (13,000 people).

Intervention: Male and female field-workers held group and personal meetings with eligible couples every two months. They used pamphlets and films for educational purposes and provided free supplies. The initial methods presented were rhythm, coitus interruptus, and foams. Condoms have been used since 1960 and sterilization since 1961.

Results: From 1961 to 1967 the birth rate in the experimental area was reduced by 12 percent and in the control area by 7 percent.

Problems/remarks: Workers were not from the villages. Preparation took a long time and only traditional methods were offered. The cost was approximately Rs60,000 (US$12,000) a year.

Reference: Population Council, "India: The Singur Study," *Studies in Family Planning*, vol. 1, no. 1 (July 1963), pp. 1–4.

Tea Estates, Assam and West Bengal

Time and place: From 1965 to 1969 in Assam and West Bengal.

Objective: To increase acceptance of family planning by offering extra incentives.

Research design: No pretest.

Intervention: Good family planning services were provided on the estates. In addition to the incentive payments usually made by the government to both acceptors and workers, the tea estates paid Rs20 (US$2.55) for sterilization plus wages for the days lost because of vasectomy or tubectomy operations. Women who received IUDs were given one to three days paid leave and medical services. Good treatment was available for side effects.

Results: The crude birth rate in Assam declined from 43.4 per thousand in 1960 to 25 per thousand in 1969. Between 1965 and 1969 there were 49,000 IUD acceptors in Assam and 9,252 in West Bengal; there was a total of 2,750 sterilizations in the two states.

Problems/remarks: There appears to be no published documentation of this scheme.

Reference: J. Oscar Alers, "Summary of Experimental Projects" (Population Council, internal memorandum, 1975).

Tea Estates (UPASI)

Time and place: An ongoing project, initiated in 1972 on the tea estates of southern India.

Institutions: United Planters' Association of South India (UPASI), government of India, and U.S. Agency for International Development.

Objective: To encourage the use of contraception by employees of three tea estates—Glendale, Bengorm, and Parkside—in southern India, by offering a delayed incentive.

Research design: Pretest.

Intervention: Mobile units bring educational activities and family planning services to the estates. Using their own records and equipment, the teams set up clinics in schools or other buildings to offer prenatal, postnatal, and child care as well as family planning. A monthly payment of Rs5 is deposited in a bank account for each woman enrolled in the program; these payments accumulate with interest as long as the enrollee does not become pregnant. At age forty-five or termination of scheme the funds become available to her. All methods except the pill have been offered. Pregnancies are detected in the course of regular health care. A participant's benefits decline with each birth; she loses all the funds if a fifth child is born.

Result: Although more than 90 percent of the eligible women enrolled during the first year, 505 of 719 enrollees were not using any form of contraception. Of the 214 women practicing a method, 75 percent accepted sterilization.

References: R. Ridker, "Savings Accounts for Family Planning. An Illustration from the Tea Estates of India," *Studies in Family Planning*, vol. 2, no. 7 (July 1971), pp. 150–52. D. Oot and M. Russell, "Family Planning Delivery Systems: An International Survey" (New York: Population Council, 1975; processed).

Indonesia

The Mojokerto Experiment

Time and place: From 1973 to 1978 in the Mojokerto regency in East Java, with a total population of approximately 619,320 in 1975.

Institutions: Government of Indonesia, World Bank, and Population Council.

Objectives: To test the feasibility of integrating maternal and child health care with family planning in rural areas of developing countries; to test whether such a combined program is an effective way to deliver family planning services and education to a large rural population.

Research design: Control/test. Mojokerto was originally designed as a demonstration project for maternal and child health, but the emphasis has now shifted to operations research. Various small experimental efforts will be tried and evaluated during the life of the project.

Intervention: The project includes both medical services and a component to evaluate the project by measuring fertility decline, coverage, and cost-effectiveness. The underlying model will also be evaluated, and the data generated by the project will be used for an international comparison of similar projects.

Results: To date there has been a series of baseline studies, including a survey of knowledge, attitudes, and practice, a study of contraceptive continuation rates, an ecological survey, and an inventory of existing rural health services and facilities. A revised service statistics system has also been completed.

Problems/remarks: Since the project was initiated, the rapid development of the national family planning program has necessitated a reassessment of how the Mojokerto project fits with the overall objectives and policies of the national program. As a result of this reassessment there has been a major modification in the relation of the evaluation component to the rest of the project. Originally intended to be autonomous, the evaluation unit is now viewed as a mechanism for providing immediate feedback on specific activities of the medical component so that medical services can be modified, if necessary, in response to the changing needs of the program. The evaluation unit will be more closely integrated into the project and will function as a monitoring mechanism for project management.

Rather than adhering closely to the Taylor-Berelson model for maternal and child health care, the Mojokerto project has turned toward operations research and will test various innovative approaches. It is no longer a contamination-free demonstration project removed from program and situational developments elsewhere in the country.

Reference: World Bank, Indonesia Project Appraisal Report no. PP-8a, February 1972, and other limited circulation reports.

International

Community-Based Distribution

Time and place: Since 1973 in several locations around the world, both rural and urban.

Institutions: The International Planned Parenthood Federation (IPPF) and the U.S. Agency for International Development have sponsored a number of community-based distribution projects, and the International Committee for Applied Research on Population (ICARP) has sponsored several commercial distribution projects.

Objective: To establish a viable, cost-effective alternative and complement to existing delivery systems for family planning services through the use of indigenous networks, both retail and nonretail, to distribute contraceptives.

Research design: The design varies according to the individual project; each one has used at least some of the following: registration, user surveys, and population surveys to evaluate operational efficiency, effectiveness, and overall impact.

Intervention: There are many variations in both the distribution networks used and the pricing policies. Contraceptives are made available through a number of household distribution schemes, through community leaders at a central depot, and from retail outlets. Prices are usually subsidized; sometimes, however, in the nonretail approach the initial supply is free and a charge is made only for the resupply. Often the distributor receives a small commission on the sale. In some experiments, the distributors are specially trained. Usually community-based distribution projects receive considerable publicity. The principal methods of contraception are condoms and pills; in some cases coupons have been distributed for subsequent IUD insertions by clinic personnel.

Result: It is difficult to measure the impact of this approach. There is a considerable substitution effect; that is, many people already practicing contraception simply switch to more readily available methods. The volume of sales can be a misleading indicator of impact and an unreliable indication of use.

References: George Washington University Medical Center, *Contraceptive Distribution—Taking Supplies to Villages and Households*, Population Reports, series J, no. 5 (Washington, D.C., July 1976). Batelle Institute, "Village and Household Availability of Contraceptives: Southeast Asia, 1976," report of a workshop held in Manila, June 1976 (Seattle, Washington, 1976; processed).

The Development and Evaluation of Integrated Health Delivery Systems (DEIDS)

Time and place: Initiated in 1972. Four demonstration areas are planned for Thailand, Pakistan, Ecuador, and an

African country still to be selected. Rural areas are the focus of the program.

Institution: American Public Health Organization, with the host country paying the local operating costs.

Objectives: To devise innovative systems for the delivery of health services and to evaluate health services in rural undeveloped areas.

Research design: Pretest.

Intervention: After identification of a site a plan is designed for each area to introduce an integrated delivery system. The pilot programs then test the feasibility of reaching at least two-thirds of the women of reproductive age and children less than five years old with services for maternal and child health care, family planning, and nutrition.

Result: The only project in operation as of 1977 was in Thailand.

Reference: American Public Health Association, Division of International Health Programs, "The Development and Evaluation of Integrated Health Delivery Systems" (Washington, D.C., undated).

Maternal and Child Health/Family Planning

Time and place: Initiated in 1974–75, the experiment is expected to extend over five years and is aimed primarily at rural areas of developing countries. Projects are underway in the Philippines, Turkey, Indonesia, and Nigeria.

Institutions: Population Council and governments of the respective countries.

Objectives: To test three hypotheses: that integrated maternal and child health/family planning programs are feasible in rural areas of developing countries and can be implemented at a reasonable and replicable expenditure of money and manpower; that the linkage between maternal and child health and family planning is mutually beneficial; and that a program based on maternal and child health care can effectively deliver family planning education and services to large populations in the rural areas of developing countries.

Research design: Pretest. General principles have been established for all projects to govern the nature of the integrated program, pilot areas, target populations, subdivision of target groups, replicability, and evaluation. For purposes of evaluation, preproject information is collected as well as service statistics on health and family planning, and there are surveys of knowledge, attitudes, and practice, registration of births and deaths, and ongoing reviews of operation. Control groups may be established.

Intervention: Contacts with mothers for family planning will be made during the antepartum period, during delivery (by professional midwives or trained birth attendants), during postpartum visits, and during child care visits. Mass media will be used to promote effective methods of contraception.

Result: The project is still in its initial stages.

Problems/remarks: The success of this program will depend on government interest.

References: Howard C. Taylor, Jr., and Bernard Berelson, "Comprehensive Family Planning Based on Maternal/Child Health Services: A Feasibility Study for a World Program," *Studies in Family Planning*, vol. 2, no. 2. (February 1971), pp. 21–54. Howard C. Taylor, Jr., and Robert J.

Lapham, "A Program for Family Planning Based on Maternal/Child Health Services," *Studies in Family Planning*, vol. 5, no. 3 (March 1974), pp. 71–82. Personal communications with Robert J. Lapham of the Population Council.

Postpartum Program

Time and place: From 1966 to 1974; initially there were 25 participating hospitals in 19 cities in 14 countries, encompassing a wide range of cultural settings. The number of participating hospitals increased during the course of the program.

Institutions: Population Council and U.S. Agency for International Development (AID).

Objectives: To provide family planning education and services to postpartum urban women of low socioeconomic status in a public hospital setting where delivery (and abortion) is institutionalized. Family planning was offered either during the hospital stay or during the first postpartum visit.

Research design: No pretest.

Intervention: In the context of the obstetrics departments of participating hospitals, the aim was to educate indigent, disadvantaged groups to raise their awareness of family planning to the level of awareness found in more advantaged groups. Brief oral presentations and visual aids were used. Each obstetrical patient was interviewed regarding demographic characteristics, contraceptive experiences, and fertility expectations. There was follow-up if a woman missed a clinic appointment. The methods offered were IUDs, rhythm, and, later in the program, pills.

Results: In 1970 AID funded a worldwide Postpartum Program follow-up survey. There were home interviews with 4,695 acceptors out of a total of 188,000 as of September 1969. The continuation rates among acceptors—for use of the first contraceptive method that they accepted—were higher than those usually observed in developing countries, and acceptors were younger and of lower parity than usual in national programs. The use effectiveness of the pill was below that of the IUD.

Problems/remarks: The international Postpartum Program is gradually being phased out; the number of participating hospitals decreased from 109 in 1972 to 54 in 1973.

References: Gerald I. Zatuchni, *Postpartum Family Planning* (New York: McGraw-Hill, 1971); and "International Postpartum Family Planning Program: Report on the First Year," *Studies in Family Planning*, no. 22 (August 1967), pp. 1–22. Irving Sivin, "Fertility Decline and Contraceptive Use in the International Postpartum Family Planning Program," *Studies in Family Planning*, vol. 1, no. 12 (December 1971), pp. 248–56; and *Contraception and Fertility Change in the International Postpartum Program* (New York: Population Council, 1974).

Iran

Isfahan Mass Communications Project

Time and place: From May 1970 to March 1971 in the entire province of Isfahan, including 515,000 people in the city of Isfahan and 1 million in rural areas. The area had experienced rapid changes and had become a diversified industrial complex—the annual growth rate for the industrial sector was 15 percent compared with 3 percent for agriculture—a trend which raised the relative cost of parenthood.

Institutions: Population and Family Planning Division of the Ministry of Health, U.S. Agency for International Development, and Population Council.

Objectives: To prepare an intensive communications campaign and to study its impact on knowledge, attitudes, and practice of family planning.

Research design: Pretest. There was a presurvey of the province between May and July 1970, and a postsurvey from April to June 1971.

Intervention: Phase I, August–November 1970: one-minute radio spots at 11:00 A.M., 12:00 noon, and 6:00 P.M. daily; five- or ten-minute announcements by various officials once a week between 6:00 P.M. and 7:00 P.M.; telephone services answered requests ten hours a day. Phase II, December 1970–March 1971: all media—radio, mailings, posters, newspapers, magazines, sound trucks, and banners—were used. IUDs and pills were offered.

Results: From three months before the campaign to three months after it, there was a net increase of 54 percent in the number of new acceptors of all methods. The campaign was evaluated in a variety of ways to determine changes in the knowledge and practice of family planning, the impact of each source of information, and the amount of discussion generated by the media. Levels of acceptance at the clinics were measured, results were compared with trends in other provinces, findings from surveys done before and after the project were contrasted, and man-on-the-street surveys were evaluated. Those who went to the clinic cited the radio as the most important source of family planning information. Friends and neighbors also ranked high as a source; newspapers and posters were less influential.

Problems/remarks: The methods offered were not permanent, which in part explains the high drop-out rate and sporadic use. The unavailability of services and supplies impeded the operation of the program (IUDs, for example, were available only in the city of Isfahan). Posters were often removed very quickly, and many of the mailings were returned because of incorrect addresses. The total cost of the project was US$8,678; if it is assumed that acceptance increased by 40 percent, the cost per new acceptor was US$2.75.

References: S. S. Lieberman, Robert Gillespie, and Mehdi Loghmani, "The Isfahan Communications Project,"

Studies in Family Planning, vol. 4, no. 4 (April 1973), pp. 73–100. Personal communications with Robert J. Lapham and Roy C. Treadway of the Population Council.

Isfahan Opinion Leaders

Time and place: From June 1970 to April 1971 in two small rural districts of Isfahan province, the shahrestans of Shahreza, 53 percent rural, and Najafabad, 42 percent rural. Each had a population of 200,000.

Institutions: Population and Family Planning Division of the Ministry of Health, U.S. Agency for International Development, and Population Council.

Objectives: To identify people who are respected in the community and to mobilize them to promote family planning.

Research design: Pretest.

Intervention: Teachers, midwives, youth corps, and village leaders were used to recruit acceptors. Only midwives received a fee, however, and this incentive was reflected in the fact that they were more successful than the other groups in recruiting. The pill and IUDs were offered.

Result: The number of users of modern methods increased from 2–3 percent to about 6 percent.

Problems/remarks: This experiment took place in the context of the Mass Communications Project.

References: S. S. Lieberman, Robert W. Gillespie, and Mehdi Loghmani, "The Isfahan Communications Project," *Studies in Family Planning*, vol. 4, no. 4 (April 1973), pp.

73–100. Personal communications with Robert J. Lapham and Roy C. Treadway of the Population Council.

Isfahan Intensive Project

Time and place: From October 1970 to December 1971 in an area within the city of Isfahan (population 9,400) and a rural area of forty-nine villages (population 8,500) in the province.

Objective: To determine whether a concentrated effort that combined the functional strategy with intensive use of the mass media and readily available contraceptive services could achieve a change in knowledge, attitudes, and practice of family planning.

Institutions: Population and Family Planning Division of the Ministry of Health, U.S. Agency for International Development, and Population Council.

Research design: Pretest. Fifteen health corps women, using 1966 census maps, identified the households, and each woman was responsible for interviewing 200 households four times during the year.

Intervention: The health corps personnel educated the households in family planning and distributed pills and condoms.

Results: Use of the pill increased from 5 to 11 percent in villages, but there was little effect in urban areas.

Problems/remarks: There were a number of operational complications such as difficulties in finding the houses and in locating women who were working in the fields. It appeared that the intensity of the project was perhaps counterproductive, and the frequency of the interviews provoked a hostile reaction toward both the project and the workers. During the second visit, which took place two months after the baseline survey, many respondents were annoyed at being asked the same questions again. On the third visit many expressed preferences for government services other than family planning. In an attempt to mollify the opposition, the fourth interview began with an apology, and the interviewer was accompanied by a nurse-midwife who could dispense pills or condoms to women who requested them. Many women also objected to being asked personal questions by young unmarried girls, and they often feared a reaction to the pill.

Reference: S. S. Lieberman, Robert Gillespie, and Mehdi Loghmani, "The Isfahan Communications Project," *Studies in Family Planning*, vol. 4, no. 4 (April 1973), pp. 73–100. Personal communications with Robert J. Lapham and Roy C. Treadway of the Population Council.

Isfahan Model Family Planning

Time and place: Between June 1972 and June 1974 in two districts of Isfahan province, 80 and 35 kilometers respectively from Isfahan city. The total population was 250,000.

Institutions: Population and Family Planning Division of the Ministry of Health, U.S. Agency for International Development, and Population Council.

Objective: To employ and to evaluate procedures for increasing the number of couples both accepting and using contraceptives.

Research design: Pretest.

Intervention: This project grew out of three other projects in Isfahan (described above) and sought to apply some of the lessons learned from them. Field-workers and opinion leaders were paid to recruit acceptors; private doctors received fees for inserting IUDs, performing sterilizations, and prescribing pills; and acceptors received compensation for traveling. The project included a variety of activities: regular visits to villages by mobile teams, integrated health and family planning services offered by clinics, group meetings, and house-to-house visits. Condoms and pills were delivered to couples at home by field-workers or were available at village stores and leaders' homes. Efforts were made to coordinate and supervise all of these activities.

Results: Knowledge of contraceptive methods was found to be almost universal. Field-workers proved to be more effective than health workers or functionaries in recruiting new acceptors. Current use by married women of reproductive age increased from 6 to 21 percent. As a result of its success, the Model Family Planning Program has been extended to twenty-six additional shahrestans (districts) covering about 3 million people (9 percent of the population of Iran). The innovative elements have still not been adopted nationwide.

Problems/remarks: The four experiments which comprise the Isfahan Mass Communications Project represent a major contribution to the field of population communication. They demonstrated that a well-planned multimedia campaign can increase the acceptance and use of contraceptives. Moreover, the Isfahan experience underscored the dictum that, if any media campaign is to be successful, it must be backed up by an adequate contraceptive delivery system. Services must be readily available and consistent with the needs of the target audience.

Even though the provincial Ministry of Health and the

Population and Family Planning Division of the national Ministry of Health endorsed the activities in Isfahan, there was no guarantee that the approaches, if successful, would be incorporated into the regular program. Other government agencies have to be convinced of the importance of experimental findings before successful approaches are adopted as part of the official program.

Reference: Roy C. Treadway, Robert W. Gillespie, and Mehdi Loghmani, "The Model Family Planning Project in Isfahan, Iran," *Studies in Family Planning*, vol. 7, no. 11 (November 1976), pp. 308–21.

Kenya

The Kenya/Kinga Experiment

Time and place: From October 1972 to November 1973 in the Meru district with a total population of 600,000 and an estimated market for condoms of 60,000 males. The average annual income was about US$220 per family; approximately 5 percent of the population had more than a primary education.

Institution: Population Services, Inc.

Objective: To discern the implications for Kenya and the donor community of social marketing—the application of commercial marketing techniques to accomplish social objectives—in a national contraceptive program.

Research design: Control only. Kirinyaga district was used as a control area.

Intervention: The name, color, and sales symbol for lubricated condoms were selected on the basis of an initial marketing survey. An aggressive advertising and sales promotion campaign was then launched using all available media (radio, cinema, and displays). Condoms were sold through village stores, and the price was subsidized. Ongoing market research was used to ascertain and monitor the reactions to the promotion.

Results: In the experimental area the current use of condoms among survey respondents increased from 4 percent before the program to 15 percent twelve months after its initiation; current use of any method increased from 21 percent prior to the campaign to 35 percent after twelve months. There was no change in the level of contraceptive use in the control area.

Problems/remarks: It is questionable whether Kirinyaga was really a suitable control area because its population was more traditional and less informed than that of Meru. The experiment demonstrated that commercial distribution of subsidized contraceptives through local outlets offers an effective avenue for reaching the rural market.

In its early stages the experiment encountered some opposition from the community. An influential physician, who operated four private rural family planning clinics, alleged that the program was selling to children. This accusation prompted local shopkeepers to become more vocal in their support of the program. Sales in Kinga were largely unaffected by the controversy, and the issue was eventually resolved.

References: Population Services International, *A Preliminary Examination of Contraceptive Social Marketing Program in Kenya* (New York, 1972). Timothy R. Black and Philip D. Harvey, "A Report on a Contraceptive Social Marketing Experiment in Rural Kenya," *Studies in Family Planning*, vol. 7, no. 4 (April 1976), pp. 101–07.

Postpartum IUD

Time and place: Specific details are unknown, but the experiment appears to have been countrywide, probably in 1973–74.

Institution: African Medical and Research Foundation.

Objective: To find out whether, with proper education, Kenyan women would accept IUDs immediately after delivery.

Research design: No pretest.

Intervention: Offering IUDs to postpartum women.

Results: No results are available.

Reference: Population Council, "Family Planning Programs, World Review, 1974," *Studies in Family Planning*, vol. 6, no. 8 (August 1975), pp. 205–324.

Korea

Cheju Household Distribution of Contraceptives

Time and place: Implemented in 1976 and expected to continue until 1979 in Cheju province, the largest island in Korea, with a population of 400,000.

Institutions: Population Institute, East-West Center, and U.S. Agency for International Development.

Objective: To increase acceptance of family planning by removing the economic, administrative, geographical, and cognitive barriers to the use of contraceptives.

Research design: Control/test. Benchmark surveys were conducted in the study area and in a control area on the mainland of Korea; there will be a postintervention survey in both areas to evaluate the efficacy and efficiency of the new delivery system in terms of increased contraceptive practice. A number of small experiments are going on simultaneously. For example, in one village the clients will be charged for pills and condoms; in another village the experiment will focus on the method of paying canvassers to determine whether their salary should be based on their performance.

Intervention: Canvassers, who received one week's training, visited all eligible households. A supply of pills for three cycles and thirty condoms were left with each couple. If a client requests a sterilization or an IUD, she is given a coupon and transportation costs to a center where the operation or insertion can be done.

Results: The experiment is still going on, and results are not yet available.

Problems/remarks: In countries like Korea with relatively well-developed family planning services, improving the availability of contraceptives might be more important than motivational services.

Reference: C. B. Park, L. J. Cho, and J. Palmore, "Household Contraceptive Distribution: Preliminary Results for Euiryong, Korea" (Honolulu: East-West Center, June 1976; processed).

Euiryong Household Contraceptive Distribution

Time and place: From May 1975 to September 1975 in three rural villages in Euiryong, a county approximately 150 kilometers northwest of Pusan. Each village had approximately 1,000 households.

Institutions: Population Institute, East-West Center, and U.S. Agency for International Development.

Objectives: To determine whether acceptance rates would be improved if economic, administrative, geographical, and cognitive barriers to contraception were removed, and to determine the most appropriate distribution system. Euiryong served as the preparatory stage for the larger experiment with household distribution of contraceptives on Cheju described above.

Research design: Control/test. Different delivery systems were introduced in each of the three villages (Yukok, Jungkok, and Koongyu). Eligible households were identified and mapped. A survey of knowledge, attitudes, and practice was conducted among eligible women, and 10 percent of the males were also interviewed. After the delivery systems had been in operation for three months a survey was conducted to measure changes in contraceptive use.

Intervention: Design I (Yukok, 100 percent method): All the households were canvassed, and those eligible were offered a supply of three 28-day cycles of pills and 30 partially lubricated condoms, attractively packaged. Written instructions explained the use of contraceptives, availability of other methods, and where and how to get additional supplies. The canvassers were mature married women living with their husbands, educated and respected by the villagers. They were trained by the crew leader (village worker) and each one covered about fifty households. They were paid attractive fees for canvassing and a modest retainer to answer questions, make referrals, and perform other minor tasks. Each canvasser was the resupply point for the households she had visited. Clients who wanted an IUD or sterilization were issued coupons and given bus fare to a nearby town for clinical treatment. Provisions were made for the possible removal of IUDs and for the care of side effects. Neither canvassers nor acceptors received any special incentives.

Design II (Jungkok, group meeting method): Group meetings for eligible women were held in the village to explain the delivery system and methods for regulating fertility.

Those wishing contraceptives were provided with the same kits of pills and condoms as those used in Yukok; those preferring an IUD or sterilization were issued coupons. Later a partial canvassing was done to reach those who had not attended a meeting.

Design III (Koongyu, 10 percent method): The clients themselves were used as canvassers. After the mapping the households were divided into groups of ten, and a woman was selected at random from each group to serve as a canvasser. The system and contraceptive methods were explained to the canvassers, but the method of distributing the supplies was left up to them. They were paid a small stipend for their activities and were supervised by two crew leaders. Other procedures were similar to the 100 percent method.

Results: Household distribution was found to be culturally, logistically, and politically acceptable. All the delivery systems increased the use of contraceptives, and their cost-effectiveness was comparable to that of the national program. In all three villages nearly 40 percent of all married women between fifteen and forty-nine years of age, living with a spouse, were using some form of contraception, an increase of 35 percent.

Problems/remarks: In comparing the three delivery systems, it was concluded that the 100 percent method was best suited to the rural Korean environment. The group method presented many administrative difficulties, and the 10 percent method required too much supervision to be cost-effective if replicated on a large scale.

This project was of relatively short duration; the Cheju experiment, scheduled to run for three years, should reveal more about trends in the use of contraceptives. In a small new project, costs are higher than in a larger long-term project where it is possible to take advantage of economies of scale. In Euiryong, the use of contraceptives in-

Table 11. Program Costs per Person Served, According to the Type of Delivery System, Euiryong Household Contraceptive Distribution Project, Korea

Village and intervention	*Total program cost*	*All receivers* (1)	*All acceptors* (2)	*Program only acceptors* (3)	*Program only current users* (4)	*Net gain users* (5)
Yukok, 100 percent	$2,809	$11.24	$16.05	$18.36	$23.21	$32.66
Number of persons		250	175	153	121	86
Jungkok, group meeting	$2,829	$10.47	$13.16	$16.07	$24.18	$39.29
Number of persons		270	215	176	117	76
Koongyu, 10 percent	$3,288	$14.11	$18.07	$23.83	$32.88	$47.65
Number of persons		233	182	138	100	69
All villages	$8,926	$11.85	$15.60	$19.28	$26.41	$39.32
Number of persons		753	572	463	338	227

Note: Columns 1–4 are based on very preliminary hand tabulations; only column 5 is based on a correct and carefully checked analysis. The column headings are defined as follows:

All receivers: all persons who accepted a contraceptive kit or who received an IUD or sterilization during the program period.

All acceptors: pill and condom users as of the postintervention survey and those who had an IUD inserted or were sterilized during the program period.

Program only acceptors: all acceptors minus those who had been using pills and condoms before the program.

Program only current users: those persons using contraceptives at the postintervention survey who had not used them before the intervention.

Net gain users: all current users at the time of the postintervention survey (including those who were users before the intervention) minus the number of users before the program's distribution.

creased dramatically among women between the ages of twenty and thirty-four, the most critical years for childbearing. It may be that greater costs are necessary to recruit younger, low-parity women. Data on costs are shown in Table 11.

Reference: C. B. Park, L. J. Cho, and J. Palmore, "Household Contraceptive Distribution: Preliminary Results for Euiryong, Korea" (Honolulu: East-West Center, June 1976; processed).

IUD Checkups

Time and place: In 1967 in Koyang county.

Institution: Yonsei University.

Objective: To determine whether retention of IUDs could be improved by special counseling to reassure the client in the early stage of use.

Research design: True experiment. At the health center, IUD acceptors were divided, more or less at random, into three groups: Tuesday's acceptors were directed to return in a week; Friday's acceptors, in two weeks; and the acceptors on the following Tuesday were told to return in one month. This produced a roughly equal distribution according to months of use among the three groups.

Intervention: Clinic checkups and counseling.

Result: An early analysis of the data disproved the hypothesis. It appeared that a visit to the clinic during the early period of stress offered more opportunity for removal, which offset the advantage of extra counseling. Retention generally improved when the follow-up visit was scheduled later.

Reference: Sook Bang, "Can IUD Retention Be Improved?" *Population and Family Planning in the Republic of Korea*, vol. 1 (Seoul: Ministry of Health and Social Affairs, Republic of Korea, March 1970).

The Koyang IUD Experiment

Time and place: A preintervention survey was made April 21 to May 8, 1965, and a postintervention survey May 1 to July 31, 1966, in six rural townships in Koyang (10,000 eligible women). As a result of the mass media campaign of the national family planning program and the use of one field-worker for each township, 10 percent of Koyang's eligible women had accepted IUDs before April 1965.

Institutions: Department of Preventive Medicine and Public Health, Yonsei University College of Medicine.

Objectives: To discern to what extent the program could be improved by making IUD services more widely available; to determine whether IUD acceptance would be affected by the sex of the doctor making the insertion; to see if insertion at any time in the menstrual cycle rather than only in the first ten days would make any difference; to determine if nurses could be used safely to insert IUDs.

Research design: Pretest. One township could be the site of multiple interventions.

Intervention: The four treatments consisted of: (a) insertion of an IUD, only in the first ten days of the menstrual cycle, in regular clinics; (b) the same as (a) except that a nurse made the insertion after a physician screened the patient; (c) insertion by a physician, at any time in the menstrual cycle; and (d) screening and insertion by nurses, at any time in the menstrual cycle. The first two treatments were offered at regular stationary clinics; the last two at a mobile service unit. Field-workers distributed educational leaflets which also listed the clinics' schedules.

Results: Because of the greater availability of services, the number of IUD insertions increased in relation to the preceding months. The sex of the doctor doing the insertion was not an important factor. In mobile clinics, if insertions were restricted to the initial ten days of the menstrual cycle, about 50 percent of the possible clients were lost. Nurses were found to be acceptable as inserters. The rate of removal—33 percent after twelve months and 52 percent after twenty-four months—was lower than the national average but equal to results in Taichung. Insertion after the tenth day of the cycle produced a somewhat higher removal rate.

Reference: Sook Bang and others, "Improving Access to the IUD: Experiments in Koyang, Korea," *Studies in Family Planning*, no. 27 (March 1968), pp. 4–11.

The Koyang/Kimpo Experiment

Time and place; From April 1962 to September 1964 in two rural villages of 8,700 and 12,000 people including, respectively, 1,400 and 1,700 married women of reproductive age. The place was selected for convenience. The population consisted mostly of farmers with little schooling and a low socioeconomic status.

Institutions: Yonsei University Medical College and Planned Parenthood Federation of Korea with the support of International Planned Parenthood Federation, Gyeonggi provincial government, and various U.S. foundations.

Objective: To assess the possibility of reducing the birth rate through family planning education and services.

Research design: Control/test. There was a baseline survey of knowledge, attitudes, and practice among 500 couples selected by systematic random sampling from the experimental and control areas. After the survey the control area, Kimpo, had no experimental intervention but did receive the normal family planning program.

Intervention: In the experimental area of Koyang field-workers taught groups of ten to fifteen women, using films and pamphlets to explain five methods of contraception: foam, condom, diaphragm, coitus interruptus, and rhythm. Individual consultation was available on request either at the clinic or at home, with monthly follow-up visits. Professional nurses were used as field-workers in this experiment. They made 100-150 calls a month. Revisits to those who initially refused a method were held to a minimum.

Results: People wanted more family planning information. In eleven months 35 percent of the eligible women were recruited, most between the ages of thirty and forty-four. Two-thirds of them (334) were still active October 1, 1963; half the dropouts were due to accidental pregnancy. The pregnancy rate for acceptors was 35.8 and for noncontraceptors 56–58 per 100 women years. The general fertility rate (controlled for age and parity) fell by 38 percent in Koyang and 13 percent in Kimpo. This experiment demonstrated the effectiveness of intensive efforts in home visits and teaching as a means of promoting contraception in rural Korea. It also showed that female workers could successfully offer a male method (the condom).

Problems: Because the control area was affected by the regular program, the comparison was actually between intensive interventions in Koyang and the regular program in Kimpo. The cost was estimated at US$15,000 a year.

References: Population Council, "Korea: The Koyang

Study," *Studies in Family Planning*, vol. 1, no. 2 (December 1963), pp. 7–9. Sook Bang and others, "The Koyang Study: Results of Two Action Programs," *Studies in Family Planning*, no. 11 (April 1966), pp. 5–12.

Mothers' Clubs

Time and place: From July 1966 to August 1967 in Koyang, a county with 143 villiages and a population of 76,810. Fifty-eight of these villages (27 experimental and 31 control) were selected for the experiment.

Institution: Yonsei University.

Objective: To evaluate the effectiveness of mothers' clubs as an educational medium for cultivating a better environ-

TABLE 12. PARTICIPATION OF VILLAGES AND OF ELIGIBLE WOMEN IN MOTHERS' CLUBS EXPERIMENT, KOYANG COUNTY, KOREA
(number)

	Low stratum[a]		*High stratum*[a]	
Group	*Villages*	*Eligible women*	*Villages*	*Eligible women*
A. Mothers' club with special educational program	7	529	6	460
B. Mothers' club with general educational program	8	1,324	6	479
Both experimental groups (A plus B)	15	1,853	12	939
C. Control; no mothers' club	18	1,963	13	963
Total	33	3,816	25	1,892

a. Low or high stratum indicates that the rate of IUD acceptance in the village was lower or higher than the average rate of its township.

TABLE 13. THE RATE OF ACCEPTANCE OF IUDS PER 100 ELIGIBLE WOMEN BEFORE AND AFTER EDUCATIONAL PROGRAM OF MOTHERS' CLUBS, KOYANG COUNTY, KOREA

	Low stratum[a]			*High stratum*[a]			*Total*		
Group	*Before*	*After*	*Total*	*Before*	*After*	*Total*	*Before*	*After*	*Total*
A. Mothers' club with special educational program	13.8	21.5	35.3	31.7	11.3	43.0	22.1	16.8	38.9
B. Mothers' club with general educational program	11.4	11.5	22.9	26.9	13.4	40.3	15.5	12.0	27.5
Both experimental groups (A plus B)									
C. Control; no mothers' club	12.1	14.4	26.5	29.3	12.4	41.7	17.9	13.7	31.6
Total	13.8	7.1	20.9	34.2	14.1	48.3	20.5	9.4	29.9

a. Low or high stratum indicates that the rate of IUD acceptance in the village was lower or higher than the average rate of its township.

ment for the acceptance and retention of IUDs and for offsetting rumors about their ill effects.

Research design: True experiment. All villages in the county were divided into two strata according to whether the IUD acceptance rate of the village was lower or higher than the average rate of its township. Experimental and control groups were randomly selected from each stratum. The number of villages and of eligible women in each group and stratum is shown in Table 12.

Intervention: The special education program for group A was conducted by family planning workers. Pictorial charts were used to explain the advantages and disadvantages of the IUD. The curriculum also included a discussion of the side effects of induced abortion. The general education program for group B consisted of routine education in family planning and maternal and child health care. Each program had a leader and one to four subordinates. They were married women, aged twenty-five to forty-five, who had more education than the village average and who had lived in the village long enough to be known and trusted by the local people.

Results: The educational program through mothers' clubs was successful in promoting acceptance of IUDs and improving their retention rate. Table 13 shows the IUD acceptance rate per 100 eligible women before and after the educational program. The program was most effective in areas that had previously had low acceptance rates. The removal rate of IUDs inserted during the study period and the reasons for removal are shown in Table 14.

Reference: Jae Mo Yang, "Use of Mothers' Clubs in Promoting IUD Acceptance and Its Effectiveness," in *Social Evaluation and Research Activities in Korea* (Seoul: Korea Sociological Association, 1972).

TABLE 14. THE RATE OF AND REASONS FOR REMOVAL OF IUDS INSERTED DURING THE STUDY PERIOD, MOTHERS' CLUBS EXPERIMENT, KOYANG COUNTY, KOREA (percent)

Months after insertion	*Pregnancy*			*Expulsion*			*Removal*		
	A	B	C	A	B	C	A	B	C
3	0.7	1.5	0.0	5.9	10.7	4.3	8.3	12.0	15.5
6	1.6	2.8	0.6	7.4	13.7	8.3	12.6	16.0	21.3
9	2.8	2.8	1.7	9.7	15.6	9.0	19.8	19.1	30.6

Note: A, B, and C refer to the experimental groups as defined in Tables 12 and 13.

Mothers' Clubs Intensity

Time and place: From 1968 to 1969 in Gyeonggi province.

Institutions: Yonsei University and Population Council.

Objectives: To ascertain whether mothers' clubs at the village level could be effective in increasing rates of acceptance and continuation of contraceptive use, and to determine whether such clubs could facilitate the field-workers' task of providing information, education, and services.

Research design: True experiment. Townships in 18 of the 19 counties of Gyeonggi province were divided into three relatively homogeneous groups in terms of population, cumulative IUD acceptance rates, number of clinics, and several socioeconomic variables. Three treatments of varying intensity were randomly assigned to each group of townships in each county: (a) one mothers' club per administrative village; (b) one mothers' club per legal village (a legal village comprises two administrative villages); and (c) no mothers' club.

A survey was conducted in December 1969 at the close of the experiment. The primary sampling unit was the county; the secondary sampling units were the enumeration districts used in the 1966 Special Demographic Survey. The questionnaire used included items concerning population characteristics as well as fertility and family planning. A total of 2,649 women who were or had been married were interviewed.

Intervention: The program was explained to community leaders, and special training was provided for leaders of mothers' clubs. Incentives were provided for mothers' clubs, although it is not clear on what basis incentives were awarded.

Results: The mothers' clubs did not appear to be effective in increasing contraceptive use or improving continuation rates, but they did facilitate the field-worker's job. The clubs provided a stable contact at the village level which was especially helpful inasmuch as the field-workers displayed a high rate of turnover.

Problems: The benefits of the mothers' club program were difficult to evaluate because of contamination of the control areas by some of the inputs of the experimental program and because frequent changes of field-workers deprived the program of continuity.

Reference: Jae Mo Yang, "Studies in Family Planning and Related Programs in Rural Korea," in *Social Evaluation and Research Activities in Korea* (Seoul: Korea Sociological Association, 1972).

Recruitment of IUD Acceptors

Time and place: 1975 in Seoul and Pusan.

Institution: International Committee for Applied Research on Population (ICARP) and Center for Population and Family Planning, Yonsei University.

Objective: To compare the performance of salaried field-workers with that of church volunteers in recruiting IUD acceptors.

Research design: No pretest.

Results: Continuation rates and satisfaction with services were similar for acceptors recruited by both field-workers and volunteers. Volunteers initially outperformed field-workers but lagged behind after eight to twelve months. They tended to recruit older women interested in terminating rather than spacing their pregnancies.

Problems/remarks: This study constitutes a strong case for further experimentation with volunteers to supplement national programs, especially in areas where the density of field-workers is low. It raises the question of how to sustain the interest of volunteers over a long period. The project was supported by an ICARP grant of US$3,860.

Reference: ICARP, "ICARP Progress Report, 1973–1975" (New York: Population Council, 1976; processed).

Seoul Agents

Time and place: January 1967 to 1968 throughout the city of Seoul.

Institution: Administered by the School of Medicine and the School of Public Health at Seoul National University.

Objective: To increase the acceptance of IUDs by using the informal communications network for recruitment.

Research design: No pretest. The design consisted simply of the intervention and the subsequent measurement of the number of acceptors. In the course of the experiment, financial constraints caused a reduction in the number of agents and facilitated a comparative evaluation of the program's impact.

Intervention: Health educators in seven of the city's nine district health centers recruited the agents who in turn recruited acceptors. In its attempt to penetrate the informal network of communications, the project used a variety of agents: housewives (whether or not they were IUD users), the chief (usually a woman) of the neighborhood, drugstore and beauty salon operators, midwives, and even a female church deacon. Some covered a regular circuit, others were positioned so that a flow of traffic came to them, and others contacted friends by their own methods. Agents originally received W50 (won) per acceptor, the health educator received W20 (in 1967, W274 = US$1.00). A three-part coupon was used to trace each acceptor from the initial contact by an agent to the insertion of an IUD.

Results: Various types of agent performed well; housewives with IUDs recruited the greatest number, but even the least effective averaged ten acceptors a month. The geographical distribution of doctors able to insert IUDs contributed to the program's success. Among the seven districts there were 46 places where a coupon could be used to obtain an IUD.

Problems/remarks: The project was so successful that funds were rapidly depleted, and in June and July 1967 the number of agents had to be reduced from twenty-one to seven in each of the districts. As the number of agents dropped, so did the number of acceptors. In September all the agents were rehired but their fee was reduced to W30.

The project operated in the context of various mass media sponsored by the national program. The agent system added the personal contact of trusted associates to the more impersonal message from the media. It is possible that the "replacement effect" was operating and that many of the acceptors would have been recruited through the regular program.

Reference: K. H. Kwon, "Use of the Agent System in Seoul," *Studies in Family Planning*, vol. 2, no. 11 (November 1971), pp. 237–40.

The Seoul Telephone Experiment

Time and place: The program began in January 1972 and lasted eighteen months in Seoul.

Institution: Planned Parenthood Federation of Korea (PPFK).

Objective: To meet the need for family planning services among a broader spectrum of the population than was being reached by the national program.

Research design: No pretest. Use was taken as a measure of effectiveness.

Intervention: Posters and news releases publicized the family planning service, which operated from 9:00 A.M. to 5:30 P.M. weekdays and 9:00 A.M. to 12:00 noon on Saturdays, closing for lunch. For the first five months a trained health educator took calls at PPFK headquarters. Later the project moved to a PPFK family planning clinic where a public health nurse answered the phone as part of her regular duties. Records were less complete after the move.

Results: Fifty-nine percent of the callers were male, most of whom wanted information on vasectomy. Over 50 percent of the calls were made from public or business phones, thus the scarcity of private phones among low-income groups did not limit the scope of the treatment.

Problems/remarks: Although a follow-up study was not possible, this was an inexpensive way of providing counseling, referrals, and information about family planning, contraception, and sex. The number of calls was correlated with the amount of publicity.

Reference: Eleanor Ching-Ching Cernada, Y. J. Lee, and

TABLE 15. THE NUMBER OF NEIGHBORHOODS AND OF WOMEN RECEIVING THE FOUR TREATMENTS OF THE SUNGDONG GU EXPERIMENT, KOREA

Treatment	*Number of neighborhoods*	*Number of women*
Mass media only	2,145	24,709
Mass media plus:		
Mailings	585	6,738
Group meetings	585	6,738
Home visits	585	6,738
Total	3,900	44,923

M. Lin, "Family Planning Telephone Services in Two Asian Cities," *Studies in Family Planning*, vol. 5, no. 4 (April 1974), pp. 111–14.

The Sungdong Gu Experiment

Time and place: From 1964 to 1966 (eighteen months) in Sungdong Gu, a section of Seoul with a total population of 370,000 in 1964. The target population was 44,900 women aged twenty to forty-four.

Institution: Seoul National University.

Objectives: To control fertility by providing the population with stimuli and motivation for an early adoption of family planning techniques; to analyze women's responses to the stimuli; and to evaluate the program's effectiveness in terms of the changes in women's knowledge, attitudes, and practice.

Research design: Control/test. There was a preintervention survey in April–June 1964 and a postintervention survey in July–August 1966. Sungdong Gu was divided into neighborhoods, each of which received one of four different treatments. A sample of 7.2 percent of the neighborhoods receiving each treatment was selected for study.

Intervention: All the married women in the neighborhoods selected were visited at home. The mass media treatment was applied to the entire area of study. Neighborhoods receiving a given treatment were scattered so that the four different treatments were evenly distributed throughout the study area (see Table 15).

Results: The rate of acceptance of family planning achieved by the use of mass media alone was 11 percent, by mass media plus mailings 12 percent, mass media plus meetings 15 percent, and mass media plus home visits 18 percent. Mass media were mentioned as a source of information by 80 percent of the survey respondents and 38 percent of the clinic visitors. Newspapers, magazines, and radio were more frequently mentioned by younger women with a higher level of education; friends, home visits, and group meetings were mentioned by older women with less education. The average cost of inducing one woman to visit the health center was W281 (about US$1.00) for mass media, W205 (US$0.75) for home visits, and W468 (US$1.70) for group meetings. No information was available on how these costs were calculated. Ordinarily one would not expect group meetings to be that much more costly than home visits.

Reference: J. Oscar Alers, "Summary of Experimental Projects" (Population Council, internal memorandum, 1975).

Malaysia

The Bidan Experiment

Time and place: A pilot project took place in six western Malaysian states from 1969 to 1974. It was expanded in 1974 to include 250 traditional midwives (*bidans*).

Institution: National Family Planning Board.

Objective: To use traditional midwives to recruit, motivate, and supply contraceptives to women whom they assisted in deliveries.

Research design: No pretest. Initially 104 midwives were selected from among the 700 who were being trained by UNICEF (United Nations Children's Fund) in 1969.

Intervention: The selected midwives were given an extra week's training and assigned to a nearby clinic. They gave their patients a card to present at the local health center where, after an examination, the patient could get an initial month's supply of pills and another coupon to exchange for more pills from the midwives.

Results: In 1973 there were 125 midwives who recruited an average of 2.1 pill acceptors a month; 77 percent of the acceptors were continuing to be resupplied after twelve months.

References: J. Y. Peng, Nor Laily bte A. Bakar, and Ariffin Bin Marzuki, "Village Midwives in Malaysia," *Studies in Family Planning*, vol. 3, no. 2 (February 1972), pp. 25–28. Everett M. Rogers and Douglas S. Solomon, "Traditional Midwives and Family Planning in Asia," *Studies in Family Planning*, vol. 6, no. 5 (May 1975), pp. 126–33.

Mexico

Postpartum/Postabortion

Time and place: From 1970 to 1972. This study was based on data on 11,076 women at five hospitals: Women's Hospital of Toluca, 1,947 women; Civil Hospital of Durango, 1,478; Civil Hospital of Guadalajara, 6,679; Tijuana Civil Hospital, 663; and the Red Cross Hospital in Tijuana, 309.

Institutions: Foundation for the Study of Population (FEPAC), a private family planning program offering subsidized services to low-income groups. There was also support from the International Planned Parenthood Federation.

Objectives: To ascertain the acceptance rates, the characteristics of acceptors according to the contraceptive method they selected, and the continuation rates of family planning delivered in this setting.

Research design: No pretest.

Intervention: Women were given a talk on family planning while they were still in the hospital after delivery or abortion. Acceptors and nonacceptors in Durango and Guadalajara were interviewed.

Results: Among acceptors the average age was twenty-seven; the majority were between twenty and thirty-four; the average number of living children per woman ranged from 3.9 to 4.6; and the rate of acceptance varied with the number of children. Orals were most frequently accepted, but injections and IUDs were also offered. Sterilization was not encouraged. The acceptors of orals were the youngest and had the least number of children (3.5).

In a study of dropouts, only 215 interviews were obtained. Those who discontinued use of the IUD tended to use some other reliable contraceptive after dropping out of the program; those who stopped using oral and injectable contraceptives did not switch to another method. When IUD acceptors were asked about their failure to return to the clinic, many said there was simply no need to return because they were satisfied with their IUD.

Problems/remarks: More and better information on family planning needs to be disseminated inasmuch as many nonacceptors held erroneous ideas about the effectiveness of a method and the incidence of side effects. About 34 percent of acceptors gave "opposition of spouse" as a reason for discontinuing a method, which indicates a need for an educational program for the spouses of postpartum and postabortion patients.

Reference: A. Keller, A. Rabago de Rodriguez, S. Correu, "The Mexican Experience with Postpartum/Postabortion," *Studies in Family Planning*, vol. 5, no. 6 (June 1974), pp. 195–200.

Traditional Birth Attendant

Time and place: From July 1974 to March 1976 in fifty villages of the Etla district of Oaxaca.

Institutions: International Committee for Applied Research on Population (ICARP) and Mexican Secretariat of Health.

Objectives: To demonstrate that it is feasible to use traditional birth attendants to motivate acceptors and resupply contraceptives.

Research design: No pretest.

Intervention: Traditional birth attendants and village volunteers were used as motivators and as sources of additional supplies of contraceptives.

Results: The approach was found to be feasible. In some villages volunteers performed better than the birth attendants, and it was recommended that each village field staff identify able and respected members of the community who would be interested in serving in addition to birth attendants. The project recommended that both birth attendants and volunteers be paid a fee for their services.

Problems/remarks: The grant from ICARP was $34,244.

Reference: ICARP, "ICARP Progress Report, 1973–1975" (New York: Population Council, 1976; processed).

Pakistan

The Lulliani Experiment

Time and place: From 1961 to 1965 in Lulliani, a primarily rural area 25 miles from Lahore, with a population of 12,500 and a crude birth rate of about 50 births per 1,000 population. Lulliani was chosen because of its proximity to a primary health center serving 50,000 people and the availability of male and female doctors and other necessary personnel. The area had been subjected to socioeconomic stress and outmigration but was similar to neighboring Punjab communities.

Institutions: Medical Social Research Project (MESOREP), Population Council, University of the Punjab, Ministry of Health. Technical direction was provided by the Department of Maternal and Child Health of Johns Hopkins University.

Objectives: To determine whether, and to what extent, an intensive program, conducted under favorable auspices and offering the best family planning methods available, could achieve acceptance sufficient to have more than a trivial impact on the birth rate; and to understand the processes through which a reduced birth rate can be achieved.

Research design: Pretest. The birth rate was measured before and after the experiment, and there were repeated surveys and continuous registration of births to enable comparison with other areas. Special surveys were conducted to show changes in knowledge, attitudes, and practice; the effectiveness of various educational approaches and methods of distribution for different groups was also studied.

Intervention: A variety of approaches was used: educational visual aids; courses for leaders and midwives; mass meetings with skits by itinerant actors; motion pictures; home visits by male and female social workers to selected married couples with three or more living children; maternal and child health care and family planning services at the health center; a network of volunteers and shopkeepers for promotion and distribution of supplies. Sterilization, IUDs, and conventional contraceptives were offered, and midwives were paid a small fee for each IUD insertion or sterilization.

Results: After thirty months, 134 IUDs were inserted for Lulliani residents. Home visits did increase the rate of acceptance, but there was a high rate of removals and expulsions. Clients came from neighboring areas as well as Lulliani, mostly as a result of word-of-mouth communication. These outsiders were not exposed to either home visits or mass publicity campaigns. No statistically significant effect on the crude birth rate of Lulliani could be attributed to the use of IUDs alone.

References: Population Council, "Pakistan: The Medical Social Research Project at Lulliani," *Studies in Family Planning*, no. 4 (August 1964), pp. 5–9. John C. Cobb and others, "Pakistan: The Medical Social Research Project at

Lulliani," *Studies in Family Planning*, no. 8 (October 1965), pp. 11–16.

The Sialkot Experiment

Time and place: From 1969 to 1971 in Sialkot a predominantly rural district but more urbanized and industrialized than most others in the country. There were about 320,000 married women of reproductive age; the total fertility rate was 8.7 in urban areas and 8.0 in rural areas.

Institution: Government of Pakistan.

Objective: To lower the population growth rate through regular and continued practice of family planning among an increasing proportion of eligible couples.

Research design: Pretest.

Intervention: One male and one female field-worker (372 in all), aged twenty-six and over, was assigned to a team to work full time in areas where they resided. Each team took a census of its area, recorded information on fecund couples, and was responsible for about 1,200 eligible couples. IUDs, pills, condoms, and sterilizations were offered. A team received a bonus for each couple who practiced family planning for one or more years without a pregnancy.

Results: The program reached about 15 percent of the eligible women. The methods offered gradually shifted from IUDs and sterilization to pills and condoms.

Problems/remarks: No sizable group of "ready" acceptors was found; most needed more motivation than could be supplied by one visit. The second visit brought in about twice as many acceptors as the first. In spite of the large inputs of money and personnel, the intensive delivery system was unable to interest a larger proportion of couples than the Lulliani program had done some years earlier. Continuation levels after one year were about equal to those of carefully controlled clinical trials. It was ascertained that followup of clients was possible in a field program that uses nonmedical personnel. The incentive system for workers proved difficult to administer and was never fully operational. In practice, the use of male-female teams was not as effective as expected because husbands were usually at work during the day and hence the usefulness of the male team member was curtailed.

References: R. Cuca and L. Bean, "Family Planning in Pakistan: A Review of the Continuous Motivation System" (Washington, D.C., 1975; unpublished manuscript). R. W. Osborn, "The Sialkot Experience," *Studies in Family Planning*, vol. 5, no. 4 (April 1974), pp. 123–29.

Peru

The Cerro de Pasco Experiment

Time and place: From 1967 to 1971 in a copper mining area in the central highlands. The population in 1971 was 34,300. The area had a high infant mortality rate and a low level of education.

Institution: This appears to have been a local effort sponsored by a mining company in the area.

Objective: To promote contraception through home visits and by increasing the availability of supplies.

Research design: Pretest. A benchmark survey of knowledge, attitudes, and practice was conducted in 1967 and a second one in 1971.

Intervention: Low-keyed advertising on radio, in newspapers, and at the cinema. Social workers employed by the mining company visited the wives of employees. A clinic offered orals, IUDs, and instruction in the rhythm method.

Results: There was about an 18 percent decline in fertility. Between 1966 and 1970 the total fertility rate fell from 8.06 children per woman to 6.58, and the general fertility rate (the number of births per 1,000 women aged fifteen to forty-nine years) fell from 244 to 203.

Problems/remarks: The change in the fertility measures cannot be attributed solely to the program.

Reference: Albert M. Marckwardt, *Findings from Family Planning Research: Latin American Supplement*, Reports on Population/Family Planning, no. 12, supplement (New York: Population Council, June 1974).

Philippines

The Paramedical Experiment

Time and place: From September 1973 to May 1974 in the Bicol region of Luzon; four rural provinces which share common languages and culture.

Institutions: International Committee for Applied Research on Population (ICARP) and Population Institute of the University of the Philippines.

Objectives: To extend family planning services into rural areas and to test the effectiveness and safety of using paramedics to prescribe oral contraceptives.

Research design: Control/test. The experimental areas (Carmines North and Carmines Sur) and control areas (Albay and Sursagon) were matched according to past performance in family planning, population size, and size of family planning staff.

Intervention: Paramedics were assigned to rural clinics under the supervision of doctors and permitted to prescribe orals. In June 1974 a survey was taken to determine the continuation rates among the paramedics' clients.

Results: As a general conclusion it was found that paramedics were a practical alternative to physicians for prescribing orals. Perhaps one of the major findings of the study was that paramedics and lay motivators had been prescribing the pills even before the experiment began. Thus the impact of the experiment was minimal because the procedure was not fundamentally new, and paramedics were probably prescribing in the control areas as well. Furthermore, the experiment attempted to compare paramedics' clients and doctors' patients who had terminated use of orals because of side effects, but the basic differences in the characteristics of the two groups make such a comparison relatively meaningless. The cost was estimated to be US$7.64 per couple year of effective protection.

Reference: James F. Phillips and Flora Bayan, "Paramedical and Lay Paramedical Prescription of Oral Contraceptives: An Experiment in the Bicol Region of the Philippines" (Manila: Population Institute, University of the Philippines, October 1974; processed).

The Philippine Telephone Experiment

Time and place: The program began in 1975 in Manila as a one-year experiment and has been continued and expanded.

Institutions: International Committee for Applied Research on Population (ICARP) and Institute of Maternal and Child Health.

Objective: To test the practicability of using the telephone service in the greater Manila area to give out information on family planning.

Research design: No pretest.

Intervention: Counselors answered questions about family planning and made referrals over the telephone in response to incoming calls.

Results: Many of the callers were young and of low parity; 42 percent were men. The counselors were able to steer general inquiries from males toward the topic of vasectomy; during one period over half the vasectomy cases in Manila were referrals from the phone service. Many calls came from public or business phones indicating that this service was reaching the less affluent population who did not own private phones. The use of public phones could also indicate a desire to preserve anonymity.

Problems/remarks: Program officials concluded that publicity for the telephone service served as another means of legitimizing family planning in Manila and provided an effective service in its own right. Officials have recommended that similar services be established in other Philippine cities. The cost was the equivalent of about US$0.34 a call.

Reference: ICARP, "ICARP Progress Report, 1973–1975" (New York: Population Council, 1976; processed).

Worker Incentives

Time and place: In 1973 in three provinces—Ilocos Sur, Pampanga, and Batangas—that represent the principal cultural groups of the northern, central, and southern regions of the island of Luzon. In each province five districts were chosen of comparable population size and density.

Institution: Philippine Commission on Population.

Objectives: To test the effect of alternative achievement quotas, payment schemes, and clinic affiliations on the performance of lay motivational workers.

Research design: Control/test. The type of quota, payment scheme, and motivator varied. Motivators were assigned a group quota, individual quotas, or no quota; they received a salary alone, a salary and bonuses, or payment per acceptor; and they either had no clinic affiliation (at large) or were clinic-based. The overall ratio of motivator to population was 1:10,000; field observations began March 1, 1973. A scoring system gave motivators two points for each acceptor of the pill or an IUD, one point for an acceptor of condoms or the rhythm method, and a half point for a remotivated acceptor.

Intervention: Five treatments were used: (a) salary only, monthly target of fifteen new acceptors per motivator, clinic-based motivators, usual record-keeping and supervision; (b) salary only, a monthly quota of 26 points per motivator, half the motivators were at large and half were clinic-based motivators, usual record-keeping and superdividual quotas, a base salary of ₱80 plus bonuses, a monthly quota of 16 points per motivator; (d) group quota (96 points per six motivators monthly), a base salary of ₱80 plus a bonus for exceeding quota; (e) no basic pay, no quota, motivators paid ₱5 a point (US$1.00 = ₱6.67 in 1973). There were two control groups.

Results: Motivators who were paid per acceptor with no quota earned the largest number of mean points; payment of bonuses plus salary had little effect on performance. Motivators at large had about four more points a month than those who were clinic-based. The data did not support the hypothesis that quotas with bonuses would yield higher performance. There were no sanctions if quotas were not met. All workers who were given incentives performed better than those receiving a salary only, but the difference was significant only for those paid per acceptor. The incidence of misreporting did not differ appreciably under any of the treatments.

Problems/remarks: The study assumed that the motivators' function was different from that of the other staff, but in actuality there was no clear distinction. It was common for incentives to be shared among staff. Motivators tended to belong to vertical rather than horizontal groups. Because they were aware that their work was being monitored, the Hawthorne effect was operative. Perhaps the most useful finding of the study was the extent to which motivators' performance was affected by such factors as poor supervision, their status in the clinic, and the informal arrangements for fee splitting. The experiment pointed out to program administrators the need for a new management system for motivators, making them independent of the authority structure of the clinic, and the need for an improved reporting system for motivators and field-workers.

Reference: James F. Phillips, A. Silayan-Go, A. Pal-Montano, "An Experiment with Payment, Quota, and Clinic Affiliations Schemes for Lay Motivators in the Philippines," *Studies in Family Planning*, vol. 6, no. 9 (September 1975), pp. 326–34.

Puerto Rico

Communication/Content

Time and place: In 1959 in twenty-three communities throughout the island.

Objective: To discern whether the educational method used to convey information on family planning would affect the level of contraceptive practice.

Research design: True experiment. Twenty-three communities having at least 100 households in a one-mile radius were randomly assigned either to one of the nine treatment groups or to a control group.

Intervention: There were three types of educational programs: Type I emphasized values, pointing out the importance of family planning and the advantages of small families, and offered information on the reproductive process and the availability of different methods of birth control. The Type II program underscored the need for sharing the responsibility for family organization in addition to offering the same information component as Type I. The Type III program encompassed all aspects of both Types I and II. In addition, each educational program was delivered in three different mediums: large meetings, small meetings, and through distribution of pamphlets only. At least two villages were randomly assigned to each of the nine possible combinations of educational program and medium.

Interviews conducted in advance were used to select couples to be included in the program. Eligible couples were distributed among four categories with respect to their attitude toward contraception: ready, uninformed, ineffective, and opposed. Another interview was conducted two months after the program, and a fertility check (interview) was conducted one year after the experiment.

Results: The impact of the program was judged in terms of the percentage of eligible couples who were contraceptive users after one year. Among those who had not previously used contraception, the values program (Type I) and the combined program (Type III) were slightly more effective than the Type II treatment; 68 percent of Type I, 63 percent of Type III, and 46 percent of Type II were using contraceptives after one year. But those who had used contraceptives at some time before the intervention responded more favorably to the Type II educational message. User rates among those who had been contraceptors were 86 percent for Type II, and 78 and 75 percent respectively for Type I and Type III treatments. The meetings and the pamphlets increased the rate of contraceptive use (both for previous contraceptors and those with no history of prior contraceptive use) over the user rates for the control groups.

Reference: Elizabeth T. Hilton and Arthur A. Lumsdaine, "Field Trial Designs in Gauging the Impact of Fertility Planning Programs," in *Evaluation and Experiment*, Carl A. Bennett and Arthur A. Lumsdaine, eds. (New York: Academic Press, 1975).

Singapore

Disincentives

Time and place: In 1972 in Singapore; the population was 2.2 million in 1973, including Chinese, Malay, and Indian ethnic groups.

Institution: Government of Singapore.

Objective: To reduce fertility.

Research design: No pretest.

Intervention: In an attempt to discourage high fertility, disincentives were introduced in 1972: higher delivery fees in the government hospital for each additional child, abolition of paid maternity leave after three children, abolition of priority for large families in the allocation of subsidized housing. In 1973 this program was intensified to include further increases in hospital delivery fees, abolition of paid maternity leave after two children, lower priority for primary school admission of fourth child and any additional, no income tax relief for fourth child and any additional, and permission for some families with three children or less to sublet government flats.

Results: Data on the degree to which women were influenced by these measures are inconclusive. They do suggest, however, that the disincentives may have affected fertility. A 1973 survey of knowledge, attitudes, and practice among married women aged fifteen to forty-four showed that three out of five of the government's disincentive policies were familiar to most. All the women surveyed thought the policies would have more influence on other people's decisions regarding family size than on their own decisions.

References: Wan Fook Kee and Saw Swee-Hock, "Knowledge, Attitudes and Practice of Family Planning in Singapore," *Studies in Family Planning*, vol. 6, no. 4 (April 1975), pp. 109–12. Saw Swee-Hock, "Singapore: Resumption of Rapid Fertility Decline in 1973," *Studies in Family Planning*, vol. 6, no. 6 (June 1975), pp. 166–69.

Sri Lanka

The Preethi Experiment

Time and place: The project began in October 1973 and covers the entire population of 13.5 million in Sri Lanka.

Objective: To increase use of condoms through subsidized sales.

Research design: No pretest.

Intervention: A major marketing campaign for a subsidized condom called "Preethi" was launched in newspapers, on radio, and at point of sale. The condoms were sold for the equivalent of US$0.04 for three and were available by mail order as well as in retail stores. In one district there were additional inputs of a health educator and ads in buses.

Results: During the first year, ending September 1974, a total of 3,432,763 condoms were sold, including 70,383 by mail order. A survey of married females showed 51 percent nationwide had heard of Preethi, and 80 percent in the experimental district. Sales leveled off to about 300,000 a month through early 1975, by rough estimate enough for approximately 2 percent of the married couples of reproductive age.

References: Population Council, unpublished appendix to Bernard Berelson and Ronald Freedman, "The Record of Family Planning Programs," *Studies in Family Planning*, vol. 7, no. 1 (January 1976). International Planned Parenthood Federation, *People*, vol. 2, no. 4 (1975).

The Sweden-Ceylon Experiment

Time and place: From 1958 to 1965 in two places: a village area twenty miles south of Colombo with a Sinhalese-Buddhist population of 6,900, and a tea estate 100 miles northeast of Colombo having 6,600 people (Indian Tamils, mostly Hindu). The village area had lower crude birth rates and crude death rates and higher literacy than did the estates.

Institutions: Governments of Sweden and Ceylon.

Objectives: To investigate prospects for family planning activities, to study attitudes toward contraception, to instruct the population in methods, and to assist in training Ceylonese public health staff in this sector.

Research design: Pretest. There was an initial attitude survey in the two areas.

Intervention: A pre- and postnatal child welfare clinic was set up in the village area. Interested women could also receive free contraceptive supplies (foam or diaphragm) from the clinic, followed two or three weeks later by a checkup. The lack of personnel made it impossible to establish a clinic in the estate area, but a mobile clinic was held there three days a week. After 1960 the program was revised to give more attention to home visits, more education to wives, and more convenient access to contraceptive supplies. In the estate areas women were permitted to receive home visits or to attend the clinic. Condoms have been available since 1961; pills since 1964.

Results: The results were not significant. The use of contraceptives was fairly low, and despite some decrease in the birth rate there was no evidence that this decline was related to the experimental treatment.

Problems/remarks: There were serious shortcomings in data collection and difficulties in recruiting staff. Because it is the custom for a woman to go to her mother's home for her first and sometimes subsequent births, it was difficult to collect data on birth registrations. The costs were estimated at US$40,000 for 1958–61 and US$70,000 after 1962; this reflects the extension of services and the opening up of new pilot areas.

Reference: Population Council, "Ceylon: The Sweden-Ceylon Family Planning Project," *Studies in Family Planning*, no. 6 (December 1963), pp. 9–12.

Taiwan

Agent Incentive

Time and place: Summer 1971, islandwide. Incentives were not new to Taiwan's family planning program; since 1966 payments had been offered to rural midwives for each referral for an IUD.

Institution: Taiwan Committee on Family Planning and Population Council.

Objective: To determine the difference in the performance of field-workers when offered a salary only and a salary plus incentives.

Research design: A true experiment, this was only one phase of a larger effort to maximize acceptance. An islandwide sample of 1,530 women who had not previously accepted contraception was selected from the participants in a 1970 study of knowledge, attitudes, and practice; 1,340 of these women in twenty counties were successfully visited. The counties were randomly divided into two groups of ten for experimental and control purposes.

Intervention: Field-workers made home visits to offer free IUD insertion, three cycles of pills, or a dozen condoms. In ten randomly selected counties field-workers received the equivalent of US$2.50 for each IUD referral and US$0.50 for each acceptor of pills or condoms in addition to their regular salary. In another ten counties field-workers received only a regular salary.

Results: In the incentive areas 6 percent of the women visited accepted an IUD and 14 percent accepted some contraceptive; excluding pregnant women and those who were already users, acceptance was 20.7 percent (457 women were visited by 37 workers). In the nonincentive areas 2 percent of the women accepted an IUD and 7 percent accepted some method; excluding those who were pregnant or already users, 10.7 percent accepted (883 women visited by 52 workers). There was an absolute increase in practice from 37.6 percent to 44.0 percent of the women visited.

Reference: M. C. Chang, G. P. Cernada, and T. H. Sun, "A Field-Worker Incentive Experimental Study," *Studies in Family Planning*, vol. 3, no. 11 (November 1972), pp. 270–72.

Contraceptive Inundation

Time and place: From April 1974 to December 1975 in twenty-four townships in Taiwan.

Institution: Taiwan Committee on Family Planning.

Objective: To assess the feasibility of household distribution of contraceptives.

Research design: Control/test. Twenty-four townships with the poorest performance in Taiwan's regular family planning program were selected and divided into twelve matched pairs, one township receiving the experimental treatment, the other continuing with the regular program. The target women were those who had registered a live birth in 1974.

Intervention: Six cycles of oral pills and six dozen condoms were provided to postpartum women. The contraceptives were distributed without charge to all target women regardless of whether they expressed desire to use them immediately. Four visits were made at regular intervals after the initial contact. By October 1975, 1,658 women had received the fourth visit.

Beginning in January 1975 in six of the twelve townships, the approach was modified to include all women aged twenty to forty-four, rather than only recent postpartum women. No followup visits were attempted; however, supply depots were set up to ensure easy accessibility to contraceptives. The modified approach has not yet been evaluated.

Results: Supplies were used by 23.5 percent of the target population; 65.3 percent of the target women were contacted, 75.5 percent of those contacted accepted supplies, and 47.7 percent of those accepting supplies used them.

From the preintervention survey in April 1974 to the time of the postintervention survey in December 1975, contraceptive use increased by 75 percent in experimental areas and by 30 percent in control areas. It should be noted that 70.2 percent of those who used the supplies had never used any other method before being contacted through the inundation approach, an indication that this approach appears to be successful with the hard-to-reach group.

Problems/remarks: The project encountered difficulties in contacting people—the list of names and addresses frequently did not coincide with the actual residence—and in providing adequate supervision of field-workers.

Reference: L. P. Chow and C. H. Yen, "The Taiwan Experience with Contraceptive Inundation," paper presented at the Conference on Village and Household Availability of Contraceptives, Manila, June 1976.

Educational Savings

Time and place: The initial enrollment took place September 1971 in Hua, a representative rural township of 35,000 people in an urban fringe. The target population was 1,089 eligible couples under thirty years of age and with three or fewer children.

Institutions: Planned Parenthood Association of China and Taiwan Provincial Family Planning Committee.

Objective: To reward those couples who limit their family size by providing funds to send their children to secondary schools and universities.

Research design: Control/test. After a baseline survey of the eligible women, a final population of 961 was selected and enrolled. A follow-up was done twelve months later and four minisurveys in December 1971 and May, October, and November 1972. The original design called for a matched group of women—drawn from surveys of knowledge, attitudes, and practice—to be studied for control purposes. It was hoped that by September 1973 researchers would be able to measure the impact of the program on the ideal of family size.

Intervention: Annual bank deposits were made for each couple, redeemable after ten to fourteen years solely for educational certificates to pay for postprimary education for their children: after fourteen years, the equivalent of US$385 for parents with one to two children; US$192 for parents with three children; zero for parents with four or more children. Free contraceptive services are provided for enrollees. There is a village follow-up for annual re-enrollment and a check against official birth registrations. In the first year there was a special program for couples with three children. People who helped with recruitment received incentives.

Results: This pilot project has met with success in terms of re-enrollment. Two-thirds of the eligible women enrolled in the initial drive; another 5 percent plus 95 percent of the initial group enrolled in the second year.

Problems/remarks: There are many unresolved issues regarding incentive schemes. It remains to be seen whether the amount paid into savings accounts is sufficient to keep families in the program and whether it is a realistic sum in view of educational costs.

References: Oliver D. Finnigan, III, and T. H. Sun, "Planning, Starting, and Operating an Educational Incentives Project," *Studies in Family Planning*, vol. 3, no. 1 (January 1972), pp. 1–7. C. M. Wang and S. Y. Chen, "Evaluation of the First Year of the Educational Savings Program in Taiwan," *Studies in Family Planning*, vol. 4, no. 7 (July 1973), pp. 157–61.

Group Meetings

Time and place: Three weeks of meetings and a six-month response period in 1964 in two townships containing both urban and rural groups. Out of about 61,000 people, 8,000 were women aged twenty to thirty-nine.

Institutions: Taiwan Population Studies Center, Taiwan Provincial Health Department, and Population Council.

Objective: To find out the difference in response between an area where all neighborhoods were given group meetings and an area where only half the neighborhoods were given meetings.

Research design: True experiment. Thirty-seven villages in two townships were randomly assigned to one of two treatments. In one treatment small group meetings were conducted by public health nurses in every neighborhood to discuss family planning; the other treatment provided for meetings to be held in only half of the neighborhoods.

Intervention: Workers visited all the women in the neighborhood who had three or more children and encouraged them to attend the meeting. At the meetings all women were given a coupon for IUD insertion.

Results: At the end of six months 381 women, 5 percent of those aged twenty to thirty-nine, had responded. Only 18 percent more women responded from areas where all neighborhoods were treated, although twice as much time was required for fieldwork.

Reference: Population Council, "Taiwan: Experimental Series," *Studies in Family Planning*, no. 13 (August 1966), pp. 1–5.

IUD Free Offer

Time and Place: Three months in 1964 in two rural townships with a combined population of 50,000.

Institutions: Taiwan Population Studies Center and Population Council.

Objective: To see if a free offer of contraceptives for a limited time would produce economic results. The usual procedure was that women would accept coupons for an IUD insertion but would have to pay the equivalent of US$0.75 for the service. At the time of this experiment only 10 percent of those accepting coupons actually visited the doctor.

Research design: True experiment. There were two treatment townships; the remaining townships on the island functioned as control groups. The measurement used was the proportion of acceptors from the target population (women aged twenty to forty-four). It is not clear whether the two rural townships were randomly selected.

Intervention: Six field-workers distributed flyers to 93 percent of the 8,080 households within six weeks. In addition to information on contraceptives, their use, and places of supply, the flyers contained a coupon for free contraceptives obtainable during a limited period. IUDs were provided at the two local health stations two afternoons a week for three months and at eight private doctors' offices in a city twenty-five kilometers away; traditional contraceptives could be obtained from a variety of places.

Results: In three months 20 percent (1,140) of the target population accepted contraceptives. The proportion of acceptors of childbearing age was higher in the experimental area than in any other of the 359 townships on the island. About 60 percent of the acceptors went to local stations to obtain an IUD rather than to the city; ten months later the retention rate was 90 percent. About 40 percent accepted condoms but only about a third were practicing after ten months. Results were better than in the regular program and also cheaper. The cost of field-worker time was the equivalent of only US$0.80 for each referral compared with US$2.50 for the islandwide program. The project was expanded to cover a large number of townships.

Reference: Population Council, "Taiwan: Experimental Series," *Studies in Family Planning*, no. 13 (August 1966), pp. 1–5.

The Kaoshiung Experiment:

Time and place: From January 1967 to May 1968 (eighteen months) in Kaoshiung, a city in the south with a population of 650,000 in 1967. Acceptance of IUDs in Kaoshiung had been among the lowest on the island, and before 1966 its family planning program had consisted of visits only.

Institutions: Taiwan Family Planning Committee, Kaoshiung City Health Bureau, and Population Council.

Objectives: To increase IUD acceptance by the active use of mass media; to introduce the pill and determine its effect on IUD acceptance; and to evaluate the use of mass media as a means of disseminating family planning information.

Research design: Pretest. In November 1966 a stratified random sample of 1,504 wives was interviewed to determine their media habits and their knowledge of family planning. A follow-up survey was made in May 1968 to determine: (a) the amount and type of exposure to family planning information from the mass media and other public information channels; (b) changes in knowledge, attitudes, and practice with respect to the pill and IUD; (c) the role of the publicity campaign in promoting change; (d) whether providing the pill to all wives lowered acceptance of the loop (IUD) over a long period. The follow-up survey reached 75 percent of the original sample. Changes in patterns of acceptance in Kaoshiung were compared with the results for the rest of the island.

Intervention: Considerable effort was put into local organization and training. Prepregnancy health workers were recruited; pill depots were set up at ten district health stations and at ten other clinics;[1] meetings were held at sixteen large factories; 55 outdoor film showings took place in the evening over six months; 1,558 letters offered free IUD insertion for a limited time only; 25,000 letters with family planning information were sent to married couples in local industry; 5,000 packets of maternal and child health care information were distributed. In January 1967 spot announcements began on the most popular women's radio program. Slides on the pill and IUD were shown in twenty-eight movie theaters; the content was informational, not motivational. The radio intervention lasted nine months, the slides three months. The eight visiting nurses who organized the effort stayed only two months, but the fieldworkers continued all year.

Results: Information and knowledge of family planning increased greatly, and there was considerable diffusion from direct to indirect receivers; people in Kaoshiung cited the mass media as a source of information more often than did those elsewhere. The current practice of contraception rose from 33 percent of the survey sample in 1966 to 42 percent in 1968; those ever practicing rose from 41 to 49 percent. Making the pill easily available had no adverse effect on loop acceptance, which rose by 16.4 percent after the pill program began in 1967. Pill acceptance reached its peak in the first year of the campaign and then declined, while IUD acceptance increased from year to year. The mass media campaign was successful, and the findings of the study were instrumental in getting the islandwide mass media campaign started in 1968.

1. One cycle of pills was sold for NT$10 (US$0.25), compared with the regular price of NT$50 (US$1.50), to anyone who had not previously bought them from a drugstore. The idea was to encourage new acceptors rather than to supply women already using the pill.

Problems/remarks: The cost was estimated at US$2,500, including salaries and public information.

Reference: George P. Cernada and Laura P. Lu, "The Kaoshiung Study," *Studies in Family Planning*, vol. 3, no. 8 (August 1972), pp. 198–203.

Mail-order Pills

Time and place: March 1964 in Taichung.

Institutions: Taiwan Population Studies Center and Population Council.

Objective: To find out if low-priced oral contraceptives could be distributed by mail.

Research design: No pretest. Pills were made available through the mail, and two self-administered questionnaires were used to determine the demographic characteristics and reproductive history of the respondents and their knowledge of family planning.

Intervention: On April 22, 1965, a two-column one-inch advertisement was put in the newspaper with a circulation of 140,000. The advertisement offered a limited supply of orals at the equivalent of US$0.50 a cycle. (The regular price in Taiwan was US$1.50.) The offer was limited to three cycles per person.

Results: In three weeks 626 requests were received, but only 531 orders were filled because of limited stock. Acceptors were better educated than the average woman. Over 70 percent wanted more children and were therefore using the pill for spacing.

Problem: There was a problem of market substitution since the surveys revealed that about half the respondents had been purchasing the pills at drugstores prior to the low-cost offer.

Reference: Population Council, "Taiwan: Experimental Series," *Studies in Family Planning*, no. 13 (August 1966), pp. 1–5.

Prepregnancy Health (Taichung)

Time and place: From February 1963 to July 1965 in the city of Taichung, with 300,000 people, of which 36,000 were women aged twenty to thirty-nine.

Institution: Provincial Maternal and Child Health Institute.

Objectives: To promote prepregnancy health and family planning; to measure the efficiency of different approaches; and to determine which measures would be realistically applicable to the island as a whole.

Research design: True experiment. The entire city was exposed to a mass media campaign, and there were four treatments with three intensities, which varied by neighborhoods within the city: (a) nothing beyond the mass media campaign and the general program; (b) mailings to two sets of couples—newlyweds and parents with two or more children; (c) group meetings, media, and personal visits to wives only; and (d) everything in (c) but to both husbands and wives. In order to test diffusion, the area of Taichung was divided into three sectors that were roughly equivalent in rural-urban distribution, socioeconomic status, and parity. The three sectors were designated at random as areas to receive high, middle, or low intensity of treatment. In the high sector 50 percent of the neighborhoods received treatments (c) and (d) in addition to the media campaign and the mailings; in the medium intensity sector 33 percent of the neighborhoods received this treatment; and in the low sector, 20 percent. The "nothing" and "mail" treatments were assigned equally to the remaining neighborhoods. In each sector the neighborhoods were assigned a treatment at random but in the indicated proportions. The impact of the program was measured before and after by a panel study of couples, case studies, and fertility statistics.

Intervention: See "Research design" above. All contraceptive methods were available. A special set of educational and informational materials was prepared for the program.

Results: Direct personal contacts produced more acceptances; visiting both husband and wife, however, had no noticeable effect. The experiment demonstrated that word of mouth was a more effective method than the mails in diffusing the message. The high-intensity areas had markedly higher acceptance rates. Overall, there was an increase in the practice of family planning and a decline in the proportion of pregnant women and in the birth rate. The IUD was the preferred method, continuation rates increased, and the retention rate was 65 percent at the end of one year. Home visits tended to produce acceptance of traditional contraceptives because the field-workers carried a supply with them. Word of mouth tended to result in acceptance of IUDs because, after being persuaded by a friend to accept family planning, a woman would go to a clinic to choose a method. Once there, she was more apt to select an IUD than a traditional method.

The initial cost per acceptor was US$4.75; after one year the cumulative cost per acceptor was down to US$3.98, and by February 1965 it was US$3.00. If all costs were assigned to IUD acceptances alone (on the assumption that other methods are not as effective as the IUD) then the comparable figures would be US$6.48; US$5.01; US$3.71. Field-workers were paid US$30 a month and supervisors US$37.50 a month.

References: Population Council, "Taiwan: The Taichung Program of Pre-Pregnancy Health," *Studies in Family Planning*, no. 1 (July 1963), pp. 10–12; and "Taiwan: The Taichung Program of Pre-Pregnancy Health," *Studies in Family Planning*, no. 4 (August 1964), pp. 10–12. R. Freedman and J. Takeshita, *Family Planning in Taiwan: An Experiment in Social Change* (Princeton: Princeton University Press, 1969).

Referral Fee

Time and place: July 1964 in a township with about 45,000 people, of which 4,500 were women aged twenty to thirty-nine.

Institutions: Taiwan Population Studies Center and Population Council.

Objective: To see if salespersons paid by the case would be less expensive than field-workers on a straight salary.

Research design: No pretest. There was neither random selection nor control groups. The impact of the intervention was measured by the number of acceptors and who referred them.

Intervention: Door-to-door salespersons were offered the equivalent of US$0.25 for each IUD case referred.

Results: After sixteen months 18 percent (808 women) of the target population had accepted an IUD. Traveling saleswomen referred about 33 percent of the cases, the general practitioners 25 percent, and previous loop cases 17 percent. The referral program was gradually expanded.

Problems/remarks: Although the results obtained by salespersons were similar to those that could be expected from a good field-worker, the cost per case (US$0.25) was substantially less than the US$2.50 for cases referred by field-workers.

Reference: Population Council, "Taiwan: Experimental Series," *Studies in Family Planning*, no. 13 (August 1966), pp. 1–5.

Taichung Spacing Program

Time and place: Begun in 1974, this ongoing program in Taichung covers all one-parity married couples, wife aged fifteen to twenty-nine, who had a first child between April 1974 and March 1975.

Institutions: Funded by a grant from International Committee for Applied Research on Population (ICARP).

Objective: To lengthen the interval between the first and second child by offering special incentives.

Research design: Pretest.

Intervention: If a second child was not born until 24–35 months after the first, the parents were offered a bonus of free delivery or NT$700 (US$18); if the second birth was 36–41 months after the first the bonus was free delivery plus free hospital care or NT$800 (US$21); if 42 months or more after the first, parents received free delivery, free hospital care, plus a free nutritional supplement or NT$900 (US$24). Field-workers received a small fee per acceptor.

Reference: Population Council, unpublished appendix to Bernard Berelson and Ronald Freedman, "The Record of Family Planning Programs," *Studies in Family Planning*, vol. 7, no. 1 (January 1976).

The Taipei Telephone Experiment

Time and place: September 1972 in the city of Taipei.

Institution: Taipei Family Planning Promotion Center.

Objective: To extend family planning services to a broader spectrum of the population than was reached by the national program.

Research design: No pretest. Use was taken as a measure of success. The intervention lent itself to neither pretest nor posttest.

Intervention: Posters and news releases advertised the telephone service, which operated from noon to 9:00 P.M. six days a week. It was run by two senior health nurses who received two weeks training prior to initiating the service; training continued while on the job. The records kept included the characteristics of the callers and their questions.

Results: Callers were 57 percent female, 43 percent male, and most frequently asked questions relating to contraception. Over 50 percent of the phone calls came from public or business phones; 20 percent of the calls at lunchtime, 35 percent in the evening.

Problems/remarks: Although follow-up was not possible, this was an inexpensive way of providing counseling, referrals, and information on family planning, contraception, and sex. The number of calls was correlated with the amount of publicity. The cost was estimated at US$0.25 a call.

Reference: Eleanor Ching-Ching Cernada, Y. J. Lee, and M. Lin, "Family Planning Telephone Services in Two Asian Cities," *Studies in Family Planning*, vol. 5, no. 4 (April 1974), pp. 111–14.

Thailand

Auxiliary Midwives

Time and place: In 1969 in seventeen provinces. There were four treatment provinces, with a total population of 2.2 million and 280,000 eligible women, and thirteen control provinces, with a total population of 8.9 million and 1.5 million eligible women.

Institution: Thai Ministry of Public Health.

Objective: To ascertain the safety of having trained midwives prescribe oral contraceptives.

Research design: True experiment.

Intervention: Auxiliary midwives who had received basic family planning training could prescribe the pill without the client having first been examined by a physician. A sample checklist was used and no pelvic examination was required.

Results: The number of pill acceptors in the treatment provinces increased fourfold in the six months after initiation of the study compared with the six preceding months.

The experimental provinces had a larger number of pill acceptors and a higher percentage of eligible women who accepted the pill than did the control areas. There was no increase in the incidence of side effects or complications when midwives prescribed the pill, and continuation rates were higher than when physicians did the prescribing.

Problems/remarks: As a result of this study, the Ministry of Public Health ruled in 1970 that the more than 3,000 auxiliary midwives throughout the country who had received basic family planning training could prescribe the pill.

Reference: A. Rosenfield and C. Limcharoen, "Auxiliary Midwife Prescription of Oral Contraceptives," *American Journal of Obstetrics and Gynecology*, vol. 114, no. 7 (December 1972), pp. 942–49.

The Chulalongkorn Experiment

Time and place: An eight-month period in 1967 at the Chulalongkorn Hospital in Bangkok, staffed with personnel from the medical school.

Institutions: Chulalongkorn University Medical School and Population Council.

Objective: To evaluate the use of special service cards to increase referrals by new acceptors of IUDs. The cards, which were valid for only two months, entitled the bearer to fast and free insertion of an IUD; they gave the name of the clinic, hours of service, and instructions to come during menstruation.

Research design: Control/test. The experimental area consisted of six widely separated provinces, two of which were matched with two control provinces before the experiment. The number of cards returned to the clinic were tabulated to get some idea of the magnitude of the direct response to the treatment. The total number of new acceptors from experimental areas, without reference to the cards returned, was compared with the number of new acceptors from other areas in order to gauge the magnitude of the indirect effect of the intervention.

Intervention: Acceptors of IUDs in the six experimental provinces were given three special service cards to distribute to friends. Cards were given to 695 women for distribution; for 26 percent of the women one or more cards were returned.

Results: In experimental provinces, average monthly insertions increased by 34 percent during the experiment; the number dropped considerably in the period after the project. In nonexperimental areas, acceptance dropped; in the two matched experimental areas, acceptance increased 28 percent and then went down. As a result of this study, special service cards were regularly distributed at Chulalongkorn Hospital.

Problems/remarks: The experiment demonstrated that the cards were used as intended and that they were perceived by the recipient as having value. It was hoped that an analysis of the cards returned would reveal what types of women were better communicators; no significant difference could be found between good communicators (one or more cards returned) and poor communicators (no cards returned).

Reference: James T. Fawcett and Aree Somboonsuk, "Thailand, Using Family Planning Acceptors to Recruit New Cases," *Studies in Family Planning*, no. 39 (March 1966), pp. 1–4.

The Potharam Experiment

Time and place: From 1964 to 1966 in a rural low-income area 80 kilometers west of Bangkok. Among the population of 75,000, 80 percent of the adults had less than four years of education, two-thirds of the women had no knowledge of contraceptives, and only about 1 percent of the population practiced family planning.

Institutions: National Research Council, Ministry of Public Health, and Population Council.

Objectives: To ascertain the acceptability of the idea of family planning and to test the readiness of rural women to practice contraception when given an acceptable method.

Research design: No pretest.

Intervention: Action began in November 1964 when contraceptive information and supplies were offered through six clinics housed in local health facilities. Two medical teams (one doctor and two nurses) staffed the clinics, spending one to four afternoons a week in each. Seven field-workers conducted educational programs through home visits and group meetings. Services were free of charge. Every third house (over 4,000 homes) was visited from November 1965 to July 1966; follow-up visits were also made. In village group meetings, film strips and flip books were used and contraceptives were distributed. Traditional midwives also were used as agents and received a small fee if a person accepted through them.

Results: Of those eligible, 20 percent accepted within eight months and 28 percent within two years. Many acceptors were from outside the district, demonstrating the effectiveness of word-of-mouth diffusion.

Problems/remarks: In spite of an outbreak of rumors about IUDs which depressed the number of new acceptors, this project paved the way for the adoption of a national family planning program. It indicated that there was substantial public interest and that the concept of family planning was acceptable to the population.

The Potharam experiment is especially notable because it included a variety of approaches to the delivery of services: clinical and extension techniques, group meetings featuring the use of media, incentives to midwives, and diffusion by word-of-mouth.

References: J. Y. Peng, "Thailand: Family Growth in Photharam District," *Studies in Family Planning*, no. 8 (October, 1965), pp. 1–7. Population Council, "Thailand and Taiwan: Program Effects after Eight Months," *Studies in Family Planning*, no. 13 (August 1966), p. 9.

Potharam Follow-up[1]

Time and place: June 1969 in a rural district of about 75,000 people. The death rate was down sharply, and although industrial technology had been introduced, the area was largely agricultural with low income.

Institution: Ministry of Public Health.

Objective: To secure information on the family planning practices of those who had accepted an IUD in the initial program (December 1964–June 1966).

Intervention: Of the original 1,161 acceptors, 902 (77.7 percent) were located and interviewed. The average accep-

1. Although this follow-up study is given separate treatment here, it is counted as part of the Potharam experiment and not differentiated in the tables and lists of the 96 experiments elsewhere in this book.

tor was twenty-four years old and had an average annual income of less than US$100.

Results: Of those interviewed, 41.8 percent still had the original IUD (34 to 53 months of use), and 51.4 percent were still practicing some other kind of contraception. After 36 months the continuation rate was 46.7 percent and after 48 months it was 41.3 percent. Present contraceptive practice was related to the number of children living: Those with two children or less had a lower rate of continued practice than did those with three or more. There were, however, no noticeable differences among continuation rates for women with three or more children. Age had no relation to present practice; the majority of women didn't want more children.

Most women had experience with only one method of contraception (IUD); very few had tried orals. Of the 902 in the sample, 43.5 percent have had one or more pregnancies since first accepting an IUD. The number of pregnancies was shown to be less than half what would have been expected during this period had there been no program.

Of women now practicing, 19.7 percent were unwilling to provide family planning information to newlyweds and young married couples; 31.7 percent of those not practicing were unwilling.

Reference: Sasichan Vimuktanon, "An IUD Follow-up Study in Potharam, Thailand," *Studies in Family Planning*, vol. 2, no. 8 (August 1971), pp. 166–70.

Time and Distance

Time and place: January 1965 to 1968 at Chulalongkorn Hospital in Bangkok. The IUD clinic was the first such program offered in a public hospital.

Institution: Chulalongkorn Medical School.

Objective: To demonstrate the way in which acceptance of the IUD was facilitated by word-of-mouth communication.

Research design: No pretest. No educational or promotional activities outside the hospital.

Intervention: IUDs were offered free at the hospital.

Results: The number of IUD acceptors in the first year (more than 12,000) exceeded by more than 10 to 1 the number of women known to have been directly informed about the program. As time passed, the number of acceptors tended to level off. Among first-year acceptors were women from 54 of the 72 provinces in Thailand. The number decreased with distance from the hospital, and this pattern continued to be characteristic over time. During the last four months of fiscal 1965, about half the cases came from outlying provinces. Distance, nevertheless, did remain a very significant factor in clinic attendance. The data did not permit an assessment of the relative importance of the factors—such as lack of information, difficulty and expense of travel—which were operating to depress rates of acceptance at greater distance. The data from clinic records did yield some information on the socioeconomic status of the acceptors. On the whole, the women were not urban, not well educated (fewer than four years of schooling), and not of excessive parity by Thai standards. The family income was less than US$30 a month.

Problems/remarks: The IUD clinic at Chulalongkorn represented a social as well as medical innovation. One of the more striking aspects of the program was the degree to which it penetrated into the rural areas. The study demonstrated the effectiveness of the process of word-of-mouth communication for the dissemination of birth control information in Thailand.

Reference: James T. Fawcett, "Thailand: Analyzing Time and Distance Factors at an IUD Clinic in Bangkok," *Studies in Family Planning*, no. 19 (May 1967), pp. 8–12.

Worker Evaluation

Time and place: From July 1971 to April 1973 in selected nonmetropolitan areas of Thailand.

Institutions: Ministry of Public Health, Chulalongkorn University, and U.S. Agency for International Development.

Objectives: To determine the most appropriate kind of field-worker for the Thai program: full-time salaried workers, workers paid incentives, or volunteers.

Research design: Control only. Study sites were selected by a three-stage sampling process. Thirty-nine workers were recruited for eleven sample areas. The target population was currently married women, aged fifteen to forty-five, living in nonmetropolitan areas of Thailand.

Intervention: Three types of workers were recruited and trained by instructors from the Maternal and Child Health Division of the Ministry of Public Health; all the recruits were female and lived in the area where they worked. They began their assignments in October 1971 and continued working until April 1973. Their main responsibility was to motivate eligible women to practice contraception.

Results: Performance was measured in terms of new acceptors and their continuation rates. It appeared that the volunteers performed the best of the three types, but the study was poorly designed and the reliability of its findings has been questioned.

Reference: Y. Porapakkham, P. J. Donaldson, G. Svetsrani, "Thailand's Field-worker Evaluation Project," *Studies in Family Planning*, vol. 6, no. 7 (July 1975), pp. 201–04.

Tunisia

Political Party

Time and Place: Initiated November 30, 1965, in two rural provinces.

Institution: Destourian political party.

Objective: To test whether the party's support would augment the practice of family planning.

Research design: Pretest.

Intervention: In the province of Beja a family planning team made periodic visits to rural areas. The Destourian party coordinated the publicity, and meetings were run by local party leaders to discuss family planning and to announce the impending visit of the team. In another province, Le Kef, clients were transported from rural areas to the central regional hospital in government vehicles. The support from the Destourian party was similar to that in Beja.

Results: The number of IUD insertions increased tremendously in both provinces, much more than in Tunisia as a whole. Acceptance in rural areas was excellent, indicating that the support of the political party was helpful.

Problems/remarks: This experiment was notable for the time it took place because it stressed the national rather than the personal benefits to be derived from adopting family planning.

Reference: Population Council, "Tunisia: The Role of the Political Party," *Studies in Family Planning*, no. 13 (August 1966), pp. 5–6.

Turkey

The Etimesgut Experiment

Time and place: From 1967 to 1975 in Etimesgut, an agricultural district consisting of eighty-three villages and two towns, west of the city of Ankara. It had a population of 65,218 in mid-1973; the average size of the villages was about 430 persons.

Institution: Institute of Population Studies at Hacettepe University.

Objectives: To provide health care for people living in the district, training facilities for medical and paramedical personnel in rural health practice, and family planning services as an integral part of the health system; to measure and evaluate the effects of an integrated health program on health and demographic changes.

Research design: Pretest. The findings from three sources were compared: 1967 and 1973 KAP surveys (knowledge, attitudes, and practice), and service statistics.

Intervention: Health and family planning services were

integrated, and both auxiliary nurse-midwives and general practitioners were used. For every 2,000 people there was one auxiliary nurse-midwife who discussed family planning, with emphasis on newer contraceptive methods, in repeated contacts with her clients. A major effort was mounted to collect vital statistics and other population data.

Results: Health conditions improved immediately, but fertility declined only after a period of three years. The total fertility rate (average number of children per woman) was 4.9 in 1967 and 4.4 in 1970 but fell to 3.4 by 1974. The 1967 KAP survey showed 50 percent as current users; by 1973, 54 percent were current users, but the most notable trend was the switch from less effective to newer, more effective methods. The improved health level in the community is attested to by the dramatic decline in infant mortality—from 142 infant deaths per 1,000 live births in 1967 to 93 in 1973—and the fall in the crude death rate from 10.3 deaths per 1,000 population in 1967 to 7 per 1,000 in 1973.

Problems/remarks: This model of a multipurpose health unit approach to the delivery of family planning services is certainly replicable on a national scale. It should be pointed out, however, that much of Etimesgut's success could be attributed to the care with which it was implemented.

Costs: It is impossible to isolate expenditures on family planning. The per capita expenditure in the health units of the Etimesgut district increased from US$2.83 in 1969 to US$3.17 in 1972.

Reference: Population Council, unpublished appendix to Bernard Berelson and Ronald Freedman, "The Record of Family Planning Programs," *Studies in Family Planning*, vol. 7, no. 1 (January 1976).

Tarsus I

Time and place: From December 1969 to July 1970. All eligible couples in eight selected villages in Tarsus, a rural district of southern Turkey with low income and education and high infant mortality.

Institutions: Development Foundation of Turkey and Institute of Population Studies at Hacettepe University.

Objectives: To determine if the distribution of conventional contraceptives through local commercial establishments would bring about increased knowledge, use, and acceptance of contraception; to ascertain if the inclusion of an educational program about family planning along with commercial distribution would have a significant additional effect on use, knowledge, and attitude.

Research design: Control/test. Four villages received free contraceptives to be distributed through commercial outlets; four other villages received commercial distribution and an educational program in family planning given separately to men and women. The design included a baseline KAP survey and a postproject survey. The same 305 women were interviewed in the initial KAP survey and the postproject survey.

Intervention: Sex-segregated group meetings were used to discuss family planning and methods of contraception. Contraceptives (condoms and vaginal foam) were distributed through village grocery stores and by local leaders.

Results: Current use increased in both groups. In villages that received an educational program (education villages) knowledge increased from 66 to 88 percent; in villages that had only free distribution of contraceptives (distribution villages) knowledge increased from 65 to 74 percent. Approval did not change in distribution villages but increased in education ones. Current users in education villages increased from 11.2 to 17.8 percent of the eligible women, a 59 percent increase; in the distribution villages current users went from 13.7 to 19 percent, a 38 percent increase. It should be noted, however, that the higher percentage increase in the education villages would have been expected, given the initially lower level of use.

Problems/remarks: The impact of education varied according to literacy, age, and length of marriage. Literate, younger, more recently married women were more likely to change.

References: Aykut Toros, "Evaluation of the Effects of an Action Program on Contraceptive Usage in Villages of the Tarsus District" (Ankara: Development Foundation of Turkey, 1970; processed). Aykut Toros and Roy C. Treadway, "The Impact of an Action Program in Family Planning: An Evaluation" (Ankara: Institute of Population Studies, Hacettepe University, 1970; processed).

Tarsus II

Time and place: From June 1971 to June 1972; eligible couples in fifty-six selected villages of the Adana-Tarsus-Mersin area.

Institutions: Development Foundation of Turkey, Institute of Population Studies at Hacettepe University, Pathfinder Foundation, and Population Council.

Objective: To observe whether contraceptive use in rural villages would increase significantly if a doctor and nurse from a nearby city were to provide family planning services on regular visits to the communities.

Research design: Control/test. There were three experimental combinations: (a) commercial distribution of condoms or vaginal tablets; (b) family planning education plus commercial distribution; (c) mobile medical units (doctor and nurse) to each village once a month with pills. A fourth group was the control. In each experimental area the villages were stratified according to socioeconomic criteria. Those of high socioeconomic status were in the plain area; those of medium status in the slope area.

Results: The percentage of eligible women using contraceptives increased from 1971 to 1972 as follows: group (a) 13 to 16 percent; group (b) 13 to 22 percent; group (c) 13 to 27 percent; and the control group 20 to 29 percent. The mobile medical units were especially effective in mountainous areas where few services were available. Areas of economic transition were most responsive to the intervention.

Problems/remarks: Because a sufficient number of doctors could not be recruited to go to the villages weekly, some of the project design had to be altered. There was some contamination of the effects from one treatment area to the adjacent area. The control area had an active family planning program sponsored by the local Family Planning Association which was not found in the other areas.

Reference: Aykut Toros, "Tarsus II: A Social Experiment in Fertility Regulation" (Ankara: Development Foundation of Turkey, 1975; processed).

Venezuela

Change Agents

Time and place: From 1972 to 1976 in Caracas and three other urban areas.

Institution: Venezuela Association for Family Planning.

Objective: To test the use of different types of change agents as motivators for the acceptance of family planning. There were formal agents of change, that is, family planning workers and health workers, and informal agents of change such as opinion leaders in the community and women who could be described as satisfied early acceptors.

Research design: Control/test. The Venezuela Association for Family Planning, using locally recruited staff, started a baseline survey in 1972, but because of political difficulties it was not completed until 1974. The baseline survey collected information on demographic and socioeconomic variables and on individual aspirations and motivations. An intensive survey of knowledge, attitudes, and practice was planned for late spring 1976 to measure attitudes, behavioral intentions, and the gap between attitudes and behavior.

Intervention: Different types of change agents were used in three of the areas and none in the control area. There were eight clinics available, two in each area.

Results: Preliminary results indicate that the peer reference group (the informal agents of change) was the most effective in recruiting acceptors.

Problems: It was difficult to define "opinion leader" and to find sufficient female opinion leaders. The results are only preliminary; a similar experiment is being undertaken in Kenya and Egypt.

Reference: Conversation with Snehendu Kar, School of Public Health, University of Michigan, October 1975.

Appendixes

Appendix A. Experiments Classified by Country or Geographical Region and Period of Initiation

Period of initiation	*India*	*Taiwan*	*Korea*	*Rest of Asia*	*Latin America*	*Africa*	*Greenland*	*International*
1950–59	Khanna Singur Madras Canvasser			Sweden-Ceylon	Communication/Content			
1960–64	Gandhigram Mehrauli Madras Community Leaders	Prepregnancy Health Group Meetings IUD Free Offer Referral Fee	Koyang/Kimpo Sungdong Gu	Dacca Lulliani Potharam Comilla Shopkeeper				
1965–69	Acceptance of Orals Narangwal Meerut Hooghly Nirodh Tea Estates, Assam and West Bengal	Mail-order Pills Kaoshiung	Koyang IUD Seoul Agents IUD Checkups Mothers' Clubs Mothers' Clubs Intensity	Field-workers Chulalongkorn Reassurance Tarsus I Etimesgut Bidan Sialkot Time and Distance Auxiliary Midwives	San Gregorio Cerro de Pasco Radio	Political Party	Greenland	Postpartum

1970–74	Tea Estates (UPASI) Andhra Pradesh Ernakulam I Ernakulam II Gujarat Ernakulam III Multipurpose Worker	Agent Incentive Taichung Educational Savings Taipei Telephone Contraceptive Inundation	Seoul Telephone Recruitment of IUD Acceptors	Worker Evaluation Tarsus II Worker Incentives Isfahan Mass Communications Isfahan Opinion Leaders Isfahan Intensive Isfahan Model Family Planning Disincentives Preethi Paramedical Mojokerto	Santo Domingo Education/Postabortion Pamphlets Change Agents Acceptor Agents PRIMOPS PROFAMILIA Rural PROFAMILIA Urban Postpartum/Postabortion Bogotá Mail/Visits SOMEFA Traditional Birth Attendant	Commodity Kenya/Kinga Danfa Postpartum IUD		Maternal, Child Health/Family Planning Community-based Distribution DEIDS
1975–79			Cheju Euiryong	Household Distribution Philippines Telephone		Experimental Home Visits		

Appendix B. Experiments Classified According to Approach Tested and Period of Initiation

Period of initiation	Personnel: Motivational: Type	Personnel: Motivational: Payment	Personnel: Clinical	Mass media	Integration	Intensive	Incentives	Inundation
1950–59	Singur Madras Canvasser Communication/Content			Communication/Content Singur		Khanna Sweden/Ceylon		
1960–64	Comilla Madras Community Leaders Prepregnancy Health Dacca Sungdong Gu Group Meetings	Referral Fee		Prepregnancy Health Sungdong Gu IUD Free Offer	Gandhigram Mehrauli	Lulliani Koyang/Kimpo Potharam		Comilla Shopkeeper
1965–69	Time and Distance Koyang IUD Field-workers Chulalongkorn		Koyang IUD	Mail-order Pills Kaoshiung Meerut Hooghly	San Gregorio Political Party Postpartum International		Tea Estates, Assam and West Bengal	Nirodh Tarsus I

	Seoul Agents Cerro de Pasco Acceptance of Orals Reassurance Bidan Sialkot Tarsus I IUD Checkups[a] Mothers' Clubs Mothers' Clubs Intensity Auxiliary Midwives			Cerro de Pasco Greenland Radio	Etimesgut Narangwal			
1970–74	PROFAMILIA Rural Isfahan Opinion Leaders Andhra Pradesh Worker Evaluation Tarsus II Santo Domingo	Worker Evaluation Worker Incentives Agent Incentive	Paramedical	Isfahan Opinion Leaders Isfahan Mass Communications Pamphlets Seoul Telephone Taipei Telephone Bogotá Mail/ Visits	Postpartum/ Postabortion Education/ Postabortion PRIMOPS Danfa Isfahan Model Family Planning Maternal, Child Health/ Family Planning	Isfahan Intensive Ernakulam I Ernakulam II Gujarat Ernakulam III	Commodity Educational Savings Tea Estates (UPASI) Disincentives Taichung	PROFAMILIA Rural Tarsus II Kenya/Kinga Community-based Distribution Preethi PROFAMILIA Urban Contraceptive Inundation

(*Table continues on next page.*)

Appendix B. *(continued)*

Period of initiation	Personnel: Motivational: Type	Personnel: Motivational: Payment	Personnel: Clinical	Mass media	Integration	Intensive	Incentives	Inundation
	Change Agents				DEIDS Postpartum IUD			
	Acceptor Agents				Mojokerto			
	Community-based Distribution							
	PROFAMILIA Urban							
	Multipurpose Worker							
	SOMEFA							
	Recruitment of IUD Acceptors							
	Bogotá Mail/ Visits							
	Traditional Birth Attendant							
1975–79	Experimental Home Visits			Philippines Telephone				Cheju Euiryong Household Distribution

a. This experiment was classified under personnel, although originally it was to test the timing of an initial return visit to the clinic after the insertion of an IUD. As the experiment developed the presence of medical personnel who could remove the IUD proved a significant factor.

BIBLIOGRAPHY

Alers, J. Oscar. "Summary of Experimental Projects." Population Council, internal memorandum, 1975.

American Public Health Association, Division of International Health Programs. "The Development and Evaluation of Integrated Health Delivery Systems." Washington, D.C., undated.

Ampofo, D. A., D. D. Nicholas, S. Ofosu-Amaah, S. Blumenfeld, and A. K. Neumann, 1976. "The Danfa Family Planning Program in Rural Ghana," *Studies in Family Planning*, vol. 7, no. 10 (October 1976), pp. 266–74.

Bang, Sook. "Can IUD Retention Be Improved?" *Population and Family Planning in the Republic of Korea*, vol. 1. Seoul: Ministry of Health and Social Affairs, Republic of Korea, March 1970.

Bang, Sook, and others. "Improving Access to the IUD: Experiments in Koyang, Korea." *Studies in Family Planning*, no. 27 (March 1968), pp. 4–11.

———. "The Young Study: Results of Two Action Programs." *Studies in Family Planning*, no. 11 (April 1966), pp. 5–12.

Bailey, Jerald. "Colombia Shows the Flag." *People*, vol. 2, no. 4 (1975).

Bailey, Jerald, and Juan Correa. "Evaluation of the PROFAMILIA Rural Family Planning Program." *Studies in Family Planning*, vol. 6, no. 6 (June 1975), pp. 148–55.

Bailey, Jerald, and María Cristina de Zambrano. "Contraceptive Pamphlets in Colombian Drugstores." *Studies in Family Planning*, vol. 5, no. 6 (June 1974), pp. 178–82.

Balakrishnan, T. R., and Ravi J. Matthai. "India: Evaluation of a Publicity Program on Family Planning." *Studies in Family Planning*, no. 21 (June 1967), pp. 5–8.

Batelle Institute, "Village and Household Availability of Contraceptives: Southeast Asia, 1976." Report of a workshop held in Manila, June 1976. Seattle, Washington, 1976. Processed.

Berg, Ole. "IUDs and the Birth Rate in Greenland." *Studies in Family Planning*, vol. 3, no. 1 (January 1972), pp. 12–14.

Black, Timothy R., and Philip D. Harvey. "A Report on a Contraceptive Social Marketing Experiment in Rural Kenya." *Studies in Family Planning*, vol. 7, no. 4 (April 1976), pp. 101–07.

Campbell, Donald J., and Julian C. Stanley. Experimental and Quasi-Experimental Designs for Research. Chicago: Rand McNally College Publishing Co., 1963.

Cernada, Eleanor Ching-Ching, J. Lee, and M. Lin. "Family Planning Telephone Services in Two Asian Cities." *Studies in Family Planning*, vol. 5, no. 4 (April 1974), pp. 111–14.

Cernada, George P., and Laura P. Lu. "The Kaoshiung Study." *Studies in Family Planning*, vol. 3, no. 8 (August 1972), pp. 198–203.

Chan, K. C. "Hong Kong: Report of the IUD Reassurance Project." *Studies in Family Planning*, vol. 2, no. 11 (November 1971), pp. 225–33.

Chang, M. C., G. P. Cernada, and T. H. Sun. "A Field-Worker Incentive Experimental Study." *Studies in Family Planning*, vol. 3, no. 11 (November 1972), pp. 270–72.

Choldin, Harvey M. "Pakistan: Shopkeeper Sales and Local Entertainment," *Studies in Family Planning*, no. 13 (August 1966), pp. 8–9.

Chow, L. P., and C. H. Yen, 1976. "The Taiwan Experience with Contraceptive Inundation." Paper presented at Conference on Village and Household Availability of Contraceptives, Manila, June 1976.

Cobb, John C., and others. "Pakistan: The Medical Social Research Project at Lulliani." *Studies in Family Planning*, no. 8 (October 1965), pp. 11–16.

Corzantes, César. *Summary of PRIMOPS Program*. School of Public Health and Tropical Medicine Technical Paper. New Orleans, Louisiana: Tulane University, February 1975, 43 pp.

Cuca, R., and L. Bean. "Family Planning in Pakistan: A Review of the Continuous Motivation System." Washington, D.C., 1975; unpublished manuscript.

Echeverry, Gonzalo. "Development of the PROFAMILIA Rural Family Planning Program." *Studies in Family Planning*, vol. 6, no. 6 (June 1975), pp. 142–47.

Faudes-Latham, Anibal, German Rodriguez-Galant, and Onofre Avendano-Portius. "Effects of a Family Planning Program in Santiago." *Demography*, vol. 5, no. 1 (1968), pp. 122–37.

Fawcett, James T. "Thailand: Analyzing Time and Distance Factors at an IUD Clinic in Bangkok." *Studies in Family Planning*, no. 19 (May 1967), pp. 8–12.

Fawcett, James T., and Aree Somboonsuk. "Thailand, Using Family Planning Acceptors to Recruit New Cases." *Studies in Family Planning*, no. 39 (March 1966), pp. 1–4.

Finnigan, Oliver D., III, and T. H. Sun. "Planning, Starting, and Operating an Educational Incentives Project." *Studies in Family Planning*, vol. 3, no. 1 (January 1972), pp. 1–7.

Freedman, R., and J. Takeshita. *Family Planning in*

Taiwan: An Experiment in Social Change. Princeton: Princeton University Press, 1969.

Gelfand, Henry M., David T. Allen, Peter S. Heller, Douglas H. Huber, Rodwin K. Nukunya, and Roger J. Poulin. "An Evaluation of the Danfa Comprehensive Rural Health and Family Planning Project in Ghana." Washington, D.C.: American Public Health Association, 1975. Processed, no. 146.

George Washington University Medical Center. *Contraceptive Distribution—Taking Supplies to Villages and Households*. Population Reports, series J, no. 5. Washington, D.C., July 1975.

Hardy, Ellen, and Karen Herud, 1975. "Effectiveness of a Contraceptive Education Program for Postabortion Patients in Chile." *Studies in Family Planning*, vol. 6, no. 7 (July 1975), pp. 188–91.

Hilton, Elizabeth T., and Arthur A Lumsdaine. "Field Trial Designs in Gauging the Impact of Fertility Planning Programs." In *Evaluation and Experiment*, Carl A. Bennett and Arthur A. Lumsdaine, eds. New York: Academic Press, 1975.

International Committee for Applied Research on Population (ICARP). "ICARP Progress Report, 1973–1975." New York: Population Council, 1976. Processed.

International Planned Parenthood Federation. *People*, vol. 2, no. 4 (1975).

Jain, Anrudh K. "Marketing Research in the Nirodh Program." *Studies in Family Planning*, vol. 4, no. 7 (July 1973), pp. 184–90.

Kee, Wan Fook, and Saw Swee-Hock. "Knowledge, Attitudes and Practice of Family Planning in Singapore." *Studies in Family Planning*, vol. 6, no. 4 (April 1975), pp. 109–12.

Keller, A., A. Rabago de Rodriguez, S. Correu. "The Mexican Experience with Postpartum/Postabortion." *Studies in Family Planning*, vol. 5, no. 6 (June 1974), pp. 195–200.

Kerlinger, Fred N. *Foundations of Behavioral Research*, 2d ed. New York: Holt, Rinehart, and Winston, 1973.

Khan, A. R., and D. Huber, 1976. "Household Contraceptive Distribution Programme in Rural Bangladesh: A Six-Month Experience," paper presented at the Conference on Village and Household Availability of Contraceptives, Manila, June 1976.

King, Timothy, and others. *Population Policies and Economic Development*. Baltimore: Johns Hopkins University Press, 1974.

Krishnakumar, S. "Kerala's Pioneering Experiment in Massive Vasectomy Camps." *Studies in Family Planning*, vol. 3, no. 8 (August 1972), pp. 177–85.

———. "Ernakulam's Third Vasectomy Campaign Using the Camp Approach." *Studies in Family Planning*, vol. 5, no. 2 (February 1974), pp. 58–61.

Kwon, K. H. "Use of the Agent System in Seoul." *Studies in Family Planning*, vol. 2, no. 11 (November 1971), pp. 237–40.

Lieberman, S. S., Robert W. Gillespie, and Mehdi Loghmani, "The Isfahan Communications Project." *Studies in Family Planning*, vol. 4, no. 4 (April 1973), pp. 73–100.

Majumdar, Murari, B. D. Mullick, A. Moitra, and K. T. Mosely. "Use of Oral Contraceptives in Urban, Rural, and Slum Areas." *Studies in Family Planning*, vol. 3, no. 9 (September 1972), pp. 227–32.

Marckwardt, Albert M. *Findings from Family Planning Research: Latin American Supplement*. Reports on Population/Family Planning, no. 12, supplement. New York: Population Council, June 1974.

Mitchell, Robert E. "Hong Kong: An Evaluation of Field Workers and Decision-Making in Family Planning Programs." *Studies in Family Planning*, no. 30 (May 1968), pp. 7–12.

Nortman, Dorothy. *Population and Family Planning Programs: A Factbook*. Reports on Population/Family Planning. New York: Population Council, 1970–75 (published annually).

Oot, D., and M. Russell. "Family Planning Delivery Systems: An International Survey." New York: Population Council, 1975. Processed.

Osborn, R. W. "The Sialkot Experience." *Studies in Family Planning*, vol. 5, no. 4 (April 1974), pp. 123–29.

Park, C. B., L. J. Cho, and J. Palmore. "Household Contraceptive Distribution: Preliminary Results for Euiryong, Korea." Honolulu: East-West Center, June 1976. Processed.

Peng, J. Y. "Thailand: Family Growth in Pho-tharam District." *Studies in Family Planning*, no. 8 (October 1965), pp. 1–7.

Peng, J. Y., Nor Laily bte A. Bakar, and Ariffin Bin Marzuki. "Village Midwives in Malaysia." *Studies in Family Planning*, vol. 3, no. 2 (February 1972), pp. 25–28.

Perkin, Gordon W. "Nonmonetary Commodity Incentives in Family Planning Programs: A Preliminary Trial." *Studies in Family Planning*, no. 57 (September 1970), pp. 12–15.

Phillips, James F., and Flora Bayan. "Paramedical and Lay Paramedical Prescription of Oral Contraceptives: An Experiment in the Becol Region of the Philippines." Manila: Population Institute, University of the Philippines, October 1974. Processed.

Phillips, James F., A. Silayan-Go, A. Pal-Montano. "An Experiment with Payment, Quota, and Clinic Affiliations Schemes for Lay Motivators in the Philippines." *Studies in Family Planning*, vol. 6, no. 9 (September 1975), pp. 326–34.

Pisharoti, K. A., K. V. Ranganathan, S. Sethu, and P. R. Dutt. *The Athoor Experience: Implications for a State-*

wide Family Planning Program. Madurai, Tamil Nadu, and Chapel Hill, N.C.: Gandhigram Institute of Rural Health and Family Planning and Carolina Population Centre, 1972.

Population Council. Unpublished appendix to Bernard Berelson and Ronald Freedman, "The Record of Family Planning Programs." *Studies in Family Planning*, vol. 7, no. 1 (January 1976).

Population Council. "Ceylon: The Sweden-Ceylon Family Planning Project." *Studies in Family Planning*, no. 6 (December 1963), pp. 9–12.

———. "India: The India-Harvard-Ludhiania Population Study." *Studies in Family Planning*, vol. 19, no. 1 (July 1963), pp. 81–96.

———. "Family Planning Programs, World Review, 1974." *Studies in Family Planning*, vol. 6, no. 8 (August 1975), pp. 205–324.

———. "Korea: The Koyang Study." *Studies in Family Planning*, vol. 1, no. 2 (December 1963), pp. 7–9.

———. "India: The Singur Study." *Studies in Family Planning*, vol. 1, no. 1 (July 1963), pp. 1–4.

———. "India: The Use of Community Leaders to Promote Family Planning." *Studies in Family Planning*, no. 13 (August 1966), pp. 6–8.

———. "Pakistan: The Medical Social Research Project at Lulliani." *Studies in Family Planning*, no. 4 (August 1964), pp. 5–9.

———. "Pakistan: The Rural Pilot Family Planning Action Programme at Comilla." *Studies in Family Planning*, no. 3 (April 1964), pp. 9–12.

———. "Taiwan: Experimental Series." *Studies in Family Planning*, no. 13 (August 1966), pp. 1–5.

———. "Taiwan: The Taichung Program of Pre-Pregnancy Health." *Studies in Family Planning*, no. 1 (July 1963), pp. 10–12.

———. "Taiwan: The Taichung Program of Pre-

Pregnancy Health." *Studies in Family Planning*, no. 4, (August 1964), pp. 10–12.

———. "Thailand and Taiwan: Program Effects after Eight Months." *Studies in Family Planning*, no. 13 (August 1966), p. 9.

———. "Tunisia: The Role of the Political Party." *Studies in Family Planning*, no. 13 (August 1966), pp. 5–6.

Population Services International. *A Preliminary Examination of Contraceptive Social Marketing Program in Kenya*. New York, 1972.

Porapakkham, Y., P. J. Donaldson, G. Svetsrani. "Thailand's Fieldworker Evaluation Project." *Studies in Family Planning*, vol. 6, no. 7 (July 1975), pp. 201–04.

Raina, B. L., Robert Blake, and Eugene M. Weiss. "India: A Study of Family Planning Communication, Meerut District." *Studies in Family Planning*, no. 21 (June 1967), pp. 1–5.

Repetto, Robert. "A Case Study of the Madras Vasectomy Program." *Studies in Family Planning*, no. 31 (May 1968), pp. 8–16.

Ridker, R. "Savings Accounts for Family Planning. An Illustration from the Tea Estates of India." *Studies in Family Planning*, vol. 2, no. 7 (July 1971), pp. 150–52.

Rogers, Everett M. *Communications Strategies for Family Planning*. New York: The Free Press, 1973.

Rogers, Everett M., and Douglas S. Solomon. "Traditional Midwives and Family Planning in Asia." *Studies in Family Planning*, vol. 6, no. 5 (May 1975), pp. 126–33.

Rosenfield, A., and C. Limcharoen. "Auxiliary Midwife Prescription of Oral Contraceptives." *American Journal of Obstetrics and Gynecology*, vol. 114, no. 7 (December 1972), pp. 942–49.

Ross, John, and others. *Findings from Family Planning Research*. Reports on Population/Family Planning, no. 12. New York: Population Council, 1972.

Ross, John, and Perry Smith. "Orthodox Experimental Designs." In *Methodology in Social Research*, H. M. Blalock and A. B. Blalock, eds. New York: McGraw Hill, 1968.

Rural Health Research Center. *The Narangwal Population Study: Integrated Health and Family Planning Services*. Narangwal, Punjab: 1975.

Simmons, Alan B. "Information Campaigns and the Growth of Family Planning in Colombia." In *Clinics, Contraception, and Communication*, J. Mayone Stycos, ed. New York: Appleton-Century-Crofts, 1973.

Sivin, Irving. "Fertility Decline and Contraceptive Use in the International Postpartum Family Planning Program." *Studies in Family Planning*, vol. 1, no. 12 (December 1971), pp. 248–56.

———. *Contraception and Fertility Change in the International Postpartum Program*. New York: Population Council, 1974.

Stoeckel, J., and Moqbul A. Choudhry. "East Pakistan: Fertility and Family Planning in Comilla." *Studies in Family Planning*, no. 39 (March 1969), pp. 14–16.

Stycos, J. Mayone, and A. Mundigo. "Motivators versus Messengers: A Communications Experiment in the Dominican Republic." *Studies in Family Planning*, vol. 5, no. 4 (April 1974), pp. 130–33.

Swee-Hock, Saw. "Singapore: Resumption of Rapid Fertility Decline in 1973." *Studies in Family Planning*, vol. 6, no. 6 (June 1975), pp. 166–69.

Taylor, Howard C., Jr., and Bernard Berelson. "Comprehensive Family Planning Based on Maternal/Child Health Services: A Feasibility Study for a World Program." *Studies in Family Planning*, vol. 2, no. 2 (February 1971), pp. 21–54.

Taylor, Howard C., Jr., and Robert J. Lapham. "A Program for Family Planning Based on Maternal/Child Health Services." *Studies in Family Planning*, vol. 5, no. 3 (March 1974), pp. 71–82.

Thakor, V. H., and Vinod M. Patel. "The Gujarat State Massive Vasectomy Campaign." *Studies in Family Planning*, vol. 3, no. 8 (August 1972), pp. 186–92.

Toros, Aykut. "Tarsus II: A Social Experiment in Fertility Regulation." Ankara: Development Foundation of Turkey, 1975. Processed.

———. "Evaluation of the Effects of an Action Program on Contraceptive Usage in Villages of the Tarsus District." Ankara: Development Foundation of Turkey, 1970. Processed.

Toros, Aykut, and Roy C. Treadway. "The Impact of an Action Program in Family Planning: An Evaluation." Ankara: Institute of Population Studies, Hacettepe University, 1970. Processed.

Treadway, Roy C., Robert W. Gillespie, and Mehdi Loghmani. "The Model Family Planning Project in Isfahan, Iran." *Studies in Family Planning*, vol. 7, no. 11 (November 1976), pp. 308–21.

Vimuktanon, Sasichan. "An IUD Follow-up Study in Potharam, Thailand." *Studies in Family Planning*, vol. 2, no. 8 (August 1971), pp. 166–70.

Wang, C. M., and S. Y. Chen. "Evaluation of the First Year of the Educational Savings Program in Taiwan." *Studies in Family Planning*, vol. 4, no. 7 (July 1973), pp. 157–61.

World Bank. Indonesia Project Appraisal Report no. PP-8a. Washington, D.C., February 1972. Limited circulation document.

Wyon, John and J. B. Gordon. *The Khanna Study*. Cambridge, Mass.: Harvard University Press, 1971.

Yang, Jae Mo. "Studies in Family Planning and Related Programs in Rural Korea." In *Social Evaluation and Research Activities in Korea*. Seoul: Korea Sociological Association, 1972.

———. "Use of Mothers' Clubs in Promoting IUD Acceptance and Its Effectiveness." In *Social Evaluation and Research Activities in Korea*. Seoul: Korea Sociological Association, 1972.

Zatuchni, Gerald I. "International Postpartum Family Planning Program: Report on the First Year." *Studies in Family Planning*, no. 22 (August 1967), pp. 1–22.

———. *Postpartum Family Planning*. New York: McGraw-Hill, 1971.

Index of Experiments

(Page numbers in boldface refer to the full description of the experiment in Part II.)

The most recent edition of *World Bank Catalog of Publications* is available without charge from:

World Bank Publications Unit
1818 H Street N.W.
Washington, D.C. 20433, U.S.A.